My Daily

WOW

Words of Wisdom

MARY GODWIN

First published in Great Britain in 2019 by MG Wisdom Publishing.

ISBN: 978 1 9162853 4 7

Cover artwork by Craig Dean Studio
Typeset by davidbushay.co.uk

www.mydailywordsofwisdom.com

DEDICATION

To my loving father and Head of the Godwin family, thank you for imparting wisdom in me from a young age through parables and storytelling your words have stayed with me and guided me through life's journey.

To my mother, greatest role model and co-leader of the Godwin clan, without your wise words and prayers this thing called life would be almost impossible to bear, thank you for your love and patience.

To my siblings, Victor and Esther, my love and respect for you increases as I see you navigate through life, thank you for your protection and admirable example.

Lastly, to my friends and family, teachers and mentors that have made life far more beautiful through your kindness, encouragement and faith, I am forever grateful.

CONTENTS

INTRODUCTION

From the time you are a child, words of wisdom are used to guide and protect you. They are used to shape and mould you into becoming the best version of yourself. And are taken from many years of experience of those before you. I have come to find that wisdom is such a crucial tool in navigating through life. But it is often reduced to common "sayings" and rarely actually applied or adhered to. It has the power to completely turn any situation in life to a more favourable outcome. There are many wise words shared often in communal forums to guide and uplift the audience. I am sure you have seen in your own life how wisdom has made a vast difference and exposed you to opportunities you dare not imagine otherwise. Wisdom can be passed on or experienced first-hand; I have encountered the benefits of both. However, it is perhaps when you are in dire need that you realise the true value of wisdom.

When I have experienced dark, lonely and devastating periods in my life I have been able to call upon the wisdom that had been shared with me. For example the wisdom given through an adage my father has shared in his effort to correct my wrong-doings. or wisdom shared through a friend or mentor, that has literally saved me, brought enlightenment and given me the strength I needed to overcome the challenge.

I am also very careful not to neglect the spiritual element that wisdom plays in our lives for we are spiritual beings as much as we are physical beings and we cannot nurture our physical, mental and emotional self without understanding that our spirit needs to be nurtured also. We may experience things in life that can literally break our spirit, so healing is a process that is necessary for us to continue to accomplish things, that we know we are born to do. I have had to heal many times from brokenness caused by life's experiences, and it is through spiritual teachings in the bible and words of wisdom passed down to me through various sources that have healed and lifted me.

When I am asked the method behind my successes whether big or small, my answer has been to apply the wisdom and tools I am exposed to daily. Not just once depending on a given scenario but every single day.

The biggest possible struggle I have found is the ability to remain consistent, consistency in pursuit of a goal, or endeavour that I know will benefit me and many others. I have stopped and started businesses, I have stopped and started diets, I have stopped and started pursuing particular career paths. But something I have learned through the wisdom that has been shared with me and the wisdom I have experienced first-hand is that every success lies in consistency and completion. And that is why I was propelled to write this book. Everything in me that has got me to where I am now is using the wisdom that is accessible and using it daily. It has guided me when I have felt lost, it has strengthened me when I have been weak, it has given me confidence when I have had none.

I know that many people can relate to a time when they have needed wisdom or are in need of wisdom right now to help them make it through. This book is for you. I have earnestly prayed and sought deep within myself to share all the words of wisdom that have guided me and are still guiding me today. I have searched deep within myself to compile words that I know will uplift, guide, challenge, encourage and motivate you.

I believe that in reading this book you will find confidence, you will heal, you will forgive, you will move on, you will be whole again, you will get that promotion, you will get out of debt, you will start and expand that business, you will write that book, you will get that contract signed, you will achieve great and marvellous things you can only imagine and much more. And I am sure of all these things because I have. And although we are different, we have more similarities than differences.

My prayer is that you will complete your life's journey, fulfil your purpose, and complete the very thing that you were not only born to do, but for which you are living and breathing in this very moment.

How to use this book
most effectively

This book is written as a daily guide. Therefore, read one 'Word Of Wisdom' a day at a time for each day of the year. You can start your Day One on any given day, however if you would like to follow the days of the year as dates on the calendar month you can use a 'Day of The Year Calendar' available via searching online or **www.mydailywordsofwisdom.com**.

There are 'Top-up' days taking into consideration the additional day provided by leap years as well as for those days where you feel you would like an extra word to lift your spirit, refocus you and set you back on track.

To get the most out of this book and increase the impact it will have on your life try not to skip any days.

Repeat the Daily WoW affirmation three times in the morning, midday and at night. This brings the words that you have read to life and is an exercise that will yield results almost instantly.

Finally enjoy reading and may your life's journey be a great success.

$\longrightarrow$

DAY 1

You are exceptionally and wonderfully created

. . .

Treasures are formed in silence and in secret places, unknown to the rest of the world. Diamonds and precious stones are processed in isolation under gruesome pressures. You are far more intricately and beautifully created, furthermore you are constantly being moulded to be the strongest and best version of yourself daily as you fuel yourself on things that nurture, nourish and grow you. It can be a lonely and a painful process but know in the end, the results will be far greater than all that you could have ever asked for or imagined. Be confident in your growth, in who you are, and who you are becoming for your very formation is excellence. You are a constant work in progress becoming more and more your complete and perfect self. Own your uniqueness and be secure in the marvel of who you are in existence.

MY DAILY WOW AFFIRMATION

I am an exceptional part of creation
I am engineered with greatness inside of me
I am not a mistake
I am becoming a better version of myself daily
I am whole and complete

DAY 2

Set goals, make a plan of action, work hard, be consistent and succeed

. . .

Pray, believe, set goals, make a plan of action to achieve those goals, work hard and be expectant that if you put the work in you will see results. Prepare for success, be grateful to everyone and everything that has contributed to your success, be kind and help others to achieve also.

This life is not guaranteed, be grateful to God the creator, for life and life in abundance. Commit your desires to God with a thankful heart and then do whatever it takes to achieve them. Do not leave the book unwritten, do not leave the job unapplied for, the business not started, the song incomplete, the country not travelled to. Be fearless in your pursuit to live a full life. Because the grave is not a respecter of persons and when it is your time to transition you want to know that you did it all with unrelenting vigour, grace and humility.

MY DAILY WOW AFFIRMATION

I am passionate about my goals
I will accomplish my plans
I am consistent
I will succeed
I am unbeatable

DAY 3

Dream big, start small

. . .

Your dreams can seem outrageous, in-comprehendible and even impossible to the average person. But the average person rarely creates innovative, life-changing, world-serving products, services or experiences, so their opinion shouldn't bother or hinder you. Fulfilling this dream may feel overwhelming and you may not know where to start. However, although the dream is big your start doesn't have to be with fireworks or a bang. Start where you are, use what you have and do what you can. If you need help, ask, if you need resources, search for them and if you need results, knock on doors of opportunity that will provide just that. Your dream is valid and it could very well be the thing that transforms the life of many now and for years to come. You've been given this dream because you have something in you that can make it happen, don't over think it, just start!

MY DAILY WOW AFFIRMATION

My dreams are possible
I have what it takes
I am innovative
I am creative
I will start and finish well

DAY 4

You have the power to sculpt and mould yourself into the masterpiece you envision

. . .

Don't let the world squeeze you into a pre-set mould. Rather, build yourself up to be exactly who you want to be. Acknowledge who you are now and understand the work that needs to be done for you to transform into the best version of yourself. The current image you have of yourself now may not be the most positive one and that is ok, because there is something you can do to change this image. What do you need to do to become a happier and healthier version of yourself? This may require you to develop your skills, sharpen your knowledge, change your environment, break bad habits, cut yourself off from relationships that no longer serve your life's purpose and remove things that do not add value to you or the person you want to become. A better you is inside of you, dig beneath the surface to discover who you truly are!

MY DAILY WOW AFFIRMATION

I love who I am becoming
I am sculpting myself for greatness
I am becoming the person I envision
I am powerful
I desire the best for myself

DAY 5

Use what is already available to you to access what is unavailable

. . .

Don't wait for it, do what you can now, with what you have, to get the resources you need, for where you want to be! You may genuinely feel like you have nothing, not a penny to your name, no reputation or contacts. If you have a mouth and can talk, ask a stranger. They are not obligated to help you, but you may just find one that is willing. And that's a start. Then keep asking until you have enough to get you to the next thing you need. What else do you have? Do you have family and friends? How can they help? If it's guidance that you need, do you have access to a library, internet or books? These are all resources rich in content to guide. Don't use what you don't have as an excuse to not go for what you could have if you just took action.

MY DAILY WOW AFFIRMATION

I have all I need to get to where I am going
Anything I lack will be provided for me
I do not lack any good thing
I am enough
I am complete

DAY 6

If you've never failed, you've never tried something new

. . .

When you try to do something that you have never done before, it can appear that failure is almost inevitable. We only know we have failed because we have an expectation of what success looks like. Failing can be vital in appreciating the true value of success. However, what is often misconstrued is the emotions attached to failure, they can be somewhat deceptive. It is not that you have failed that is significant, it is that you have made an attempt at success and you are significantly closer than you were before you made that attempt, and with each attempt you are even closer to succeeding. With this knowledge you then realise the importance of continuing to make new attempts. Therefore not concentrating on the failure but focusing on getting closer to success, learning how you can attempt better or try another way until you eventually succeed.

MY DAILY WOW AFFIRMATION

I welcome new opportunities into my life
I am not afraid of trying something new
I am not afraid of failure
I am constantly learning how to be better
I learn from my past failures

DAY 7

Do not allow fear to block you from a great opportunity

. . .

There is so much waiting for you on the other side of that door of opportunity. Don't find comfort in darkness because you are used to it. Don't be afraid to step into the unknown, you have everything inside of you that you need to make it work, even if all you have is a tiny mustard seed sized faith. Fear is a liar and only portrays things in a negative light, often excluding the positives. It encourages negative emotions attached to failure or shame as opposed to positive emotions attached to accomplishment and a sense of pride for overcoming a challenge. It is ok to be presented by fear and to even feel fear, but don't let it block or imprison you, especially when what lies beyond is endless opportunities for growth, promotion, and elevation.

MY DAILY WOW AFFIRMATION

I am not afraid to succeed
I am not afraid to fail
I welcome the right opportunities
The right doors are opening for me
Greatness awaits me

DAY 8

Love yourself enough to want better and to be better

. . .

Love liberates! Be able to love yourself enough to not settle for less than you are worth, that is the most rewarding gift you can give to yourself and those around you. You are worthy of love, especially self-love, you owe it to yourself to deeply care about the things that concern you and your future. Yes, you may have made mistakes, failed miserably, let yourself or those around you down. But it's important to forgive yourself, and believe that you can do better. It's important to believe that you can change and invest in that change. It is also important to give yourself a second, third and fourth chance as you may need some time to get it right. Be patient with yourself, don't be your own task master ready to bring out the whip if you get things wrong. Coach, encourage and sponsor your own growth. And with time you will get to where you want to be.

MY DAILY WOW AFFIRMATION

I love myself enough to want the best for myself
I am worthy of every blessing
I will not settle for less than the best
My self-love liberates me
I am improving daily

DAY 9

Don't give up, the beginning is always the hardest

. . .

It can be easy to want to put off something that you know involves your full effort, focus and determination, with no guarantee that it will yield the results you even want. Do not be deterred. Just start, no matter how small and no matter how slowly you go. Do whatever is necessary to get the ball rolling. Make the call, send the email, start writing, start producing, pick up the paint brush, book that ticket, get in the car, knock on that door, take the first step and keep walking until you are strong enough to run. You will find that once you get started things will take off and you'll find a rhythm that will keep you going. And if you don't find it the first time keep starting until you do find it. It's ok to start more than once. There are no rules for getting it done. Just get it done.

MY DAILY WOW AFFIRMATION

I will not be overwhelmed
I will not give up
I will keep on going
I will push through
I am resilient

DAY 10

Your health is an investment not an expense

. . .

One of your biggest investments and one of the most important investments you can ever make is in yourself!

Your health is so important! In fact, one of the most reputable books in the world, gives reference to your body being a temple. A place, beautifully adorned and recognised as a Holy Place of worship. Therefore, you should treat it as such. You can only do and give what your body and mind allows you to. You are only as good as your investment in yourself mentally, physically, emotionally and spiritually. So be your best by giving yourself your best. This shouldn't feel like a chore or a burdened cost that deprives you from self-indulgence, but rather a seed of empowerment that will yield long lasting results. You will never regret investing in your improvement in fact you will thank and love yourself for it!

MY DAILY WOW AFFIRMATION

My health is important to me
I am becoming healthier in all areas of my life
I am choosing healthier options
I am doing what is best for my health
I am much healthier now

DAY 11

Respect yourself enough to let go of anyone who doesn't see your worth

. . .

Don't ignore the signs, some people are in your life for a reason and a season. It may be your season to move on from something or someone that no longer is fit for purpose. It is all a part of life; the world is constantly in motion and so are people. You can choose to continue to follow the same people, however if their path is in a different direction to your destination then you are only moving further away from where you are meant to be going. It is better to let go and to press on towards your desired goal, because the cost of forsaking your own path to hold on to someone, is that you end up in a completely different place in life to that which you know you should be, which can result in a lot of associated problems that could have easily been avoided.

MY DAILY WOW AFFIRMATION

I am whole and complete
I do not require validation from anyone
I am enough
I am precious
I add value because I am valuable

DAY 12

The time is now

. . .

Don't delay! Stop waiting, contemplating, deliberating, or second guessing! You have enough information to start and if you feel like you don't, use the information that you have now to acquire the information that you will need to continue. But what you must do is start. Start where you are, start with what you have, start with what you know and with who you know. Yes, you have to be practical, but you can also be flexible and willing to adapt. Things are forever changing and evolving, be willing to learn and improve over time. If you are waiting for a sign, you are the sign! The light is green, and the arrow is pointing forward. Be at peace all you need to do is start, the answers will come, the help will come, the knowledge will come, and the opportunities will come. The time is now.

MY DAILY WOW AFFIRMATION

I am taking action now
I will not procrastinate
I will not waste time
I am efficient
I start and finish well

DAY 13

You don't have to be great to get things started but you have to start to be great

. . .

The cost of greatness is being willing to take that leap of faith and just start. When the promise is clear the price is reasonable and with greatness the promise is held in starting and not stopping until you reach your destination. The price paid will be insignificant once you receive your reward and there is no prerequisites as you obtain and gain all you need along the way. If you fall or fail, stand up gracefully, dust yourself off and continue or start again if you have to. It will get easier with time, you will get more confident in your ability, you will be more experienced and will gain foresight on what not to do or how to do things better next time. And in time you will have enough understanding so you can begin to teach others, therefore paving the way for those that come after you.

MY DAILY WOW AFFIRMATION

I will not delay starting
I will start great
I will complete what I have started
I will continue despite having setbacks
I am an awesome starter and finisher

DAY 14

Success is on the other side of sacrifice

. . .

If you had to make a known but doable sacrifice in order to accomplish a set goal you want to achieve, would you do it? What if it was the body of your dreams? A job of a lifetime? Becoming a successful global business owner? Would you make the sacrifice and commit to it every day to achieve your goal?

What is certain is time will pass, what is not guaranteed is what you will become if you are not willing to give something to gain everything. The price is insignificant when the vision is clear!

It is important to take certain risks, make certain sacrifices and do things most people are not willing to do. When you have a clear vision of the promise at the end of all the hard work, the reward is far greater than the temporary discomfort.

MY DAILY WOW AFFIRMATION

I am willing to make sacrifices
I am committed to the vision
I am disciplined
I have self-control
I will see my vision through to the end

DAY 15

What is your motivation

. . .

Many people have goals, but it is not always clear what the reason for the goal is. To pursue a goal with no or little intention makes it very difficult to be motivated to achieve the goal. Being intentional with your ambition for success gives life and awakens passion. It makes it less like ticking off a to do list and more like fulfilling purpose. Purpose is a great driving force to achieving any endeavour. So, what is the intention behind your aspirations? What is the driving force that ignites your passion to succeed? Who do you want to be? Whose life do you want to impact? What legacy do you want to leave for those coming up behind you? What small steps can you take that will come together to form your ultimate goal? Let all these things be your motivation.

MY DAILY WOW AFFIRMATION

I am motivated to win
I am passionate about succeeding
I am intentional with my goals
I am impactful
I am pursuant

DAY 16

Step out of your comfort zone

. . .

To get impactful and long-lasting results will sometimes require more from you than what you are used to producing. By stepping out of your comfort zone and challenging yourself you expand your capacity and elevate your reach. Staying within your comfort zone can stunt growth and often leaves you in a state of contentment where you feel like you have reached your optimum level. The difficulty is the bar is always being raised and the goal post always moved further away. The limit is endless, so by not moving you are actually regressing. By stepping out of your comfort zone, you step into limitless potential for more, greater and better things in life. And stepping out doesn't mean you can never have moments of solace or live a life where you constantly feel out of your depth, it merely is a way to prepare for enlargement and progress.

MY DAILY WOW AFFIRMATION

I am confident
I am adventurous
I am not afraid to take risks
I am breaking barriers
I am limitless

DAY 17

Don't despise small beginnings

. . .

Big things often have small beginnings. In fact, an example of this in nature is a mustard seed. One of the smallest seeds that when planted and grown over time becomes one of the biggest trees. It has countless ways in which it is used by society including, food, shelter, fuel and the list continues. When you have a vision or goal that is great, do not be discouraged that you have to start small. Don't get frustrated about how long it will take or overwhelmed by how much work you will need to put in before you yield any results. No matter what it takes, just be consistent! Sometimes the path is rocky, sometimes it bends way to the left, sometimes it looks impossible and your destination seems further away. But if you continue you will never regret it, you will get closer and closer until you finally get there!

MY DAILY WOW AFFIRMATION

I welcome growth into my life
Better things are coming
I am encouraged
I start expectant of success
I have peace that everything will work out

DAY 18

Don't stress over things you cannot control

. . .

The reason why you may often be stressed or overwhelmed is because you are trying to control the things you have no control over, this can sometimes make you feel powerless, defeated or affect your self-esteem. However, it is often hard to control what people think of you, what they say to you, how they decide to treat you, what they do to you, what they tell others about you. Even if it is unmerited someone can treat you in a way that seems unfair. Despite all of this, what you can absolutely control is yourself and your actions. Ultimately when you master yourself and your response, you can influence those around you to do and be better, to treat you better, to think better and to say better things. Rather than stress over your lack of control, take control of what you can control.

MY DAILY WOW AFFIRMATION

I have peace
I am grateful for what I have
I am expectant of great things to come
I make well thought through decisions
I do not act on fear
I act on faith

DAY 19

Step out in faith

. . .

At times you may be challenged to walk by faith and not by sight. If you are ever in a situation where things are uncertain, but you are required to take action in order to be afforded the opportunity to be in a more promising position, take that step of faith. Do whatever is necessary to tune into a system of belief that on the other side of the unknown is something better. This level of faith may mean that you demand more from yourself, you may need a response from your other senses, so depend more on your hearing, touching, tasting and smelling capabilities. Stop focusing on what you do not have, use what is in your possession, which you will realise is far more than what you think you lack. You have everything you need to start, you just need to be willing to take that initial step.

MY DAILY WOW AFFIRMATION

I walk by faith
I have peace things will work out
I trust my journey
My steps are divinely directed
I turn my plans into action

DAY 20

Believe in your future self

. . .

Everything you will be, is counting on everything that you are right now. And to get there you must believe that you can and that you will. In fact everything is relying on your determination to be all that you set out to be, to have all that you set out to have and for you to get all that you set out to get. There is no question of a doubt, this is simply fact that hasn't caught up with reality. And although it may surprise many, you will not be surprised because you always knew that you would do it. Your confidence in yourself is based from an inward source, powered by purpose. Your faith is fuelled by a will carved into your DNA. You are becoming more of yourself, who you will be and are destined to become by faith and your belief.

MY DAILY WOW AFFIRMATION

I believe in the person I am becoming
I do not let doubt discourage me
I am powered by purpose
I am fuelled by destiny
I believe I am becoming my best self

DAY 21

It may not get easier, but you get stronger

. . .

Every time you take on a difficult project and you are able to push pass the initial hardship that is involved in getting started, you break boundaries through sheer determination. Powering through challenges despite the mental opposition with the hope that one day you will get better, you build muscle, physical and mental muscle. You also develop willpower, that acts as strength to keep going until you reach your desired endpoint. That willpower will get you up early in the morning, or staying up until very late, it makes you go the extra mile even if every fibre in your body is desiring you to stay exactly where you are. You have the power to be exactly who you want by making the right investments in yourself. You are the creator of your own destiny and it may not be an easy journey, but you will power through if you stay with it.

MY DAILY WOW AFFIRMATION

I am becoming stronger daily
I am becoming better
I have great willpower
I am not lazy
I am hard working

DAY 22

Pray, work hard and be patient

. . .

There is power in centring yourself with creation through the creator. Meditating on a desired outcome and committing it to a power bigger than yourself. Then taking action through faith by working hard towards your desired objective. Be relentless in achieving, by constantly putting your energy in seeing your desired outcome through, and don't stop until you see it established. Whilst you work hard be at peace that it is coming and this may mean you waiting, but don't stop putting in the work. In this instance patience really is a virtue, it's only a matter of time before everything you've been working so hard for behind the scenes will yield results and finally take you to places you can only dream of or imagine!

MY DAILY WOW AFFIRMATION

I trust my process
I know things are working out for me
I am committed to working hard
I do not act in haste
I know what awaits me is great

DAY 23

Stop doubting yourself, you can do it so get it done

. . .

There are things in life you want to achieve, you've seen others do great things and it has inspired you to aim high. If they can do it, why can't you? If they can overcome challenges, break through barriers, smash glass ceilings, why can't you? You have all you need to accomplish your vision, if you didn't, it wouldn't be engraved in your heart and mind.

Stop doubting yourself and start or continue taking those steps that bring you closer to where you want to be. Be relentless in your pursuit of greatness, be relentless in your quest to fulfil purpose. You were born for such a time as this, for such a cause as this. What is in you is like none other, your DNA is the evidence of this. Do not doubt your ability. Put in the work. Do not give up and you will see greatness unfold before you.

MY DAILY WOW AFFIRMATION

I believe in myself
I have great ability
I am skilled
I am hardworking
I am relentless

DAY 24

Be willing

. . .

The will to change, the will to commit, the will to wait, the will to put in the work. It starts with a willing heart, a desire to be more than what you are now, the inclination to put your faith into action. With will you stir up a determination within yourself to make it happen. Simply wanting something in your heart is enough to transform your mind, enough to make you act. With willingness you can see your goals through to the end. Be willing to make changes in your life for the better. Be open to the idea that it can be done and you can be the one to do it. And not only can it be done, but it will be done and you will be the one to do it. Your will to do something sparks a fire in your heart to create nothing into something.

MY DAILY WOW AFFIRMATION

I am determined
I put my faith in action
I know my efforts will yield results
I will not give up
I am willing to commit to my journey

DAY 25

Faith over fear

. . .

Be hopeful about the unknown rather than afraid of something that is unreal, that has not even happened yet, or is possibly unlikely to ever happen. Wait in excitement and anticipation for something great to unfold, for your dreams to manifest and for your blessings unimaginable to come to pass. Do not be held in bondage to lies conceived in darkness. Let faith rise up within you as a light guiding you to a great and expected end. Let faith give you the freedom to choose joy, to choose love, to choose peace, to choose hope. Do not sit down waiting or expecting for the worst to happen, instead be expectant to see the best in life and in people. Faith triumphs over fear every time, so choose faith every time, it will lead you to places you have only dreamt of.

MY DAILY WOW AFFIRMATION

Fear will not stop me
I am confident that I will overcome
I act in faith
I trust my process
I am hopeful

DAY 26

First you must believe

• • •

It is great to have some sort of goal, vision or plan for your life. But what is your expectation of the end result? Do you earnestly expect your goal to be reached? Your vision to be realised? Your plan to be executed? To see it happen you must believe. You must be certain of the unknown, to have hope that the outcome will be exactly what you expect it to be. Faith can be given or created, belief can be formed by you changing the way you think and by developing your mind. You are what you think, you are what you believe you are. See your goals, visions and plans as the truth, know and be sure that it can be done, and you will be the one to do it. This is the start of creating a solid foundation for what you are hoping for.

MY DAILY WOW AFFIRMATION

My faith is unshakeable
My vision is clear
I believe in myself
I am capable of great things
I have expectations of success

DAY 27

You deserve the best

. . .

No matter what do not settle! You deserve the best! The best for yourself first, so that you can be more effective in giving your best to others. Do not let anyone short change you or rob you of what is rightfully yours and even more importantly don't cheat yourself out of your best, by not recognising your value or worth. You are worthy, you are valuable, you are a masterpiece and when you receive the best into your life, you maintain and increase your value. When you are valuable you add value to those around you, you are able to impart worth into others, you are able to see more in people than they see in themselves, just by virtue of them being associated with you. Be in environments that bring out your best, where you thrive and shine. Be the best, do your best, give your best!

MY DAILY WOW AFFIRMATION

I deserve the best
I will give myself my best
I will do my best
I will perform at my best
I will strive for excellence

DAY 28

Don't tell people your dreams show them

. . .

Your dreams can excite you to the point where you want to shout them and sing them from the mountain top, however this is not always necessary. In fact you shouldn't feel the need to explain, justify, or convince anyone about your goals, visions or dreams. It is a God-given gift that you have for the world. It contributes to your purpose, character and identity. It is far too precious to disclose casually, rather treasure it and hold it dear to your heart. Guard it with all your heart and work on it with all your might. It will manifest in time and will speak for itself. Sometimes sharing it prematurely with people that may not fully understand, could kill, steal or delay things. Be protective of your vision as they are the offspring of your deepest desires. Once they are formed, they can bring you unspeakable joy and fulfilment.

MY DAILY WOW AFFIRMATION

I am gifted

My dreams are valid

I will see my dreams through

I will protect my dreams

I will realise my dreams

DAY 29

Love never fails

. . .

Love conquers, redeems, liberates, brings joy and gives life. It is possibly the most powerful driving force there is in life. It is more than likely that the power of love cannot be truly grasped. If all else fails and you feel like all hope is gone, look for love. You will find it in a smile, a hug, a heart-warming memory, laughter, amongst friends and family or a past-time. Why? Because it is the unexplainable reason and foundation for all these things. Many things are uncertain, but love is sure, it is to be experienced and shared, to be shown and spread. Love can give strength you never knew you had, love can give you a deep joy to forget your sorrow, love can even heal you. Love in everything you do, let it be the force that motivates you and navigates you in the direction of purpose.

MY DAILY WOW AFFIRMATION

I will love myself more
I will act from a place of love
I will be motivated by love
I am worthy of love
My love is valuable

DAY 30

Push through

. . .

Pushing requires you to lean into what you want to move. What are you looking to shift? Change direction of? Or move forward? In order to do it, you need to lean into it, put your whole self into it and apply effort. For more affect it may require all of you. What obstacles are in your way? Pushing through is not a passive act, you have to be intentional. You have to know what you want to change and where you want to go. You can't let the weight of what hinders you, deter you. You are stronger than the obstacle. You have what it takes to build momentum and to complete the task at hand. Give it all you have and don't stop until it is finished. You are built with what is required and as you do what you must, you become stronger.

MY DAILY WOW AFFIRMATION

I will not give up
I will keep going until I win
I will push through the pain
I will break through the barriers
I will overcome the obstacles

DAY 31

You only lose when you quit

. . .

It's not over until you win! Stop throwing in the towel and stop giving up. Get up. Show up. Show out. Get those results. You haven't worked this hard to have nothing to show at the end of it. You are not a loser so you can't quit. You are not a failure so you can't give up. Keep on going, give it all you have and even when you feel like you have nothing left, draw from your reserve. Command more from yourself. You have it in you to succeed, push through, keep pushing, even if it looks impossible, there is a promise of success at the end. Tune into your belief system to give you strength to commit to the cause. You cannot let yourself down. Do not miss out on the opportunity that can change the entire trajectory of your life if you just remain pursuant.

MY DAILY WOW AFFIRMATION

I will not quit
I will win
I will not throw in the towel
I will commit to finishing
I will complete my journey

DAY 32

It is ok to restart

. . .

Make an honest evaluation of yourself, if what you are doing is not working and hasn't been working for a while, don't stick with it because you don't want to seem like a failure. It's time to move on. If you are depreciating rather than seeing a return on your investment. Don't lose everything before you realise it is time to pull out. Learn your lessons and apply it to future endeavours. You do not have to be ashamed if something did not work out. You are doing more than an observer, making unwarranted comments. Only because you haven't succeeded yet, it doesn't mean that you won't succeed. You have found a better way to get to your final destination. The most important thing is that you get there. So, don't give up trying even if it means you have to start again.

MY DAILY WOW AFFIRMATION

I will evaluate my current status
I am committing to the best for myself
I will start well
I will stay devoted to my vision
I always find my way to success

DAY 33

You can do ALL things through Christ who gives you strength

. . .

This sounds like a very loaded religious statement taken from the bible and it somewhat is. Whether you are religious or not the very example that this historic figure gives in demonstrating resilience, love, mercy, faith, willpower and grace, should motivate and give you strength. Understanding the challenges, he had to endure to give hope to many, so that they could believe and stand against adversity is powerful in and of itself. He believed that everything he did, anyone having hope and belief in his ability could do what he did and more. Knowing this should give you courage and confidence. You can, because Jesus believes you can and his spirit lives in you through your faith. And even if you feel at your weakest a perfect strength will rise within you. Be confident that the challenges you faced have been conquered once before and with faith you can use that same strength to conquer them again.

MY DAILY WOW AFFIRMATION

I receive my strength from a divine source
I achieve more with God
There is nothing impossible for God
I am blessed
I am favoured

DAY 34

Stop doubting yourself you have what it takes to make it happen

. . .

It's very easy to be your own harshest critic, but what you have to realise is not all of those negative voices you hear inside of your head come from you. And furthermore, when you hear those doubts or negative voices you don't have to take them on. You really don't know what you can or cannot do because you are constantly growing and evolving. Something that was difficult and impossible before, you now do with ease. Think about walking, what if as a toddler you looked at all the people around you and doubted that you could ever do that because every time you tried you fell. Instead you kept trying until you finally walked. Cultivate that same willpower and mind-set. If you put the work in, you will definitely get results. So, stop doubting and start doing what it takes.

MY DAILY WOW AFFIRMATION

I do not doubt my ability
I am capable of great things
My hard work pays off
I am constantly growing
I am getting better each day

DAY 35

Winners are not people who do not fail, but people who do not quit

. . .

There are times when you can feel tempted to throw in the towel and give up. You may want to stop pursuing your goals, dreams, visions and decide to procrastinate by delaying until next month or next quarter.

However, what you may not realise is that you've subconsciously told yourself it's ok to quit for now and start again later. Quitting is the easiest option and when you decide to go with the easy option, your body, mind and soul automatically resist the harder, more difficult option next time around. Hence why most New Year resolutions don't work, because you are already programmed in your subconscious to quit when it gets hard. Don't give in, don't give up, don't quit! See beyond today, see the reward and the pay-off for all the hard work you put in when you decided to remain consistent.

MY DAILY WOW AFFIRMATION

I win because I refuse to quit
I am committed to winning
I am determined
I am resilient
I will not stop until I win

DAY 36

Don't pay attention to the naysayers

. . .

You may have negative people who will try to discourage you, to limit your elevation for fear of your elevation, and when they can no longer manipulate you, they may try to manipulate the perception others have of you. This can feel hurtful especially when the person trying to bring you down is close to you. but find solace in your integrity. Don't be persuaded to justify yourself. Trust that the people that are really for you, will eventually see the truth just like you did. The truth is there is power and beauty in silence. Let your vision of the future be so clear, that everything that does not align to it is just background noise. Your focus is what ultimately shapes who you are. Focusing on the negative things people say or think about you, only fuels insecurity, poor judgement and distrust.

MY DAILY WOW AFFIRMATION

I focus on the prize
I do not acknowledge negativity
I think positively
I do not get distracted
I stay on track

DAY 37

Start with you

. . .

It's so easy at the beginning of the year to make new year resolutions to improve external factors, such as a goal to lose weight, get fit, be more organised, more punctual, save or make more money.

But these things won't change unless you change and what I mean is change your mind set, your perception of yourself, your character the essence of who you are. Unless you work on this and give yourself time to truly put these things in check, that long list of resolutions will be just that, a list. There is only very little you can change externally if internally you are still the same. The same way of thinking is going to yield the same results it has always yielded and that clearly is not much. Take time to think about the person you want to become, then adapt the mind-set needed to become exactly that.

MY DAILY WOW AFFIRMATION

I am becoming mentally stronger
I am committed to building a good foundation
I am constantly developing
I am building good character
I am improving in everyway

DAY 38

Stop being afraid of what could go wrong and start being positive about what could go right

. . .

Fear is so deceptive because it creates an undesirable scenario that has not happened and that is unlikely to happen. However, this image alone, generates negative emotions which hinder you from taking any action towards a possible outcome. In taking no action you feel in control, like you've spared yourself humiliation from the worst thing that could have happened. When in actual fact you may have limited yourself from obtaining the best. Rather than thinking the worst possible scenario, think of the best that could happen, that on the other side of your effort lies a great reward, a gift, a congratulations for your great success or taking a chance and going for it. Even if it doesn't work out like you expected, that moment will pass, failure is temporal, it is not final. There is a higher chance that next time you will succeed, so think just that.

MY DAILY WOW AFFIRMATION

I walk by faith not by fear
I am confident of my success
I am motivated by faith
I am not worried
I expect positive results

DAY 39

Look how far you have come

. . .

It is so important to take stock of yourself, to be reflective of your successes and areas where you may have not done so well. Take time to celebrate and praise yourself for overcoming that challenging situation, or learning from that mistake. Make a mental note of where you slipped, where things went wrong, which paths are better left alone and which paths are best to take. Observe your growth, admire the things you now leap over, which were once mountains you had to climb. There is something significant about taking a look at how far you've come that motivates you to keep pressing on. It equips you with what you need for the onward journey, using lessons, clothing yourself with confidence and not being weighed down by doubt in your capacity or your ability to eventually reach your goal. So look with pride, you have come a long way.

MY DAILY WOW AFFIRMATION

I am proud of my achievements
I celebrate my successes
I am doing a great job
I will continue to do well
I am growing day by day

DAY 40

Be excited about your transformation

. . .

The fact that you are not where you used to be, you have changed and grown, even if it is just in the most subtle of ways, this is reason enough to get excited. Excited about your development and excited about how much more you can be more than what you are now. You are not who you used to be. You are better, stronger and wiser, equipped with more knowledge that you have acquired by just living through your experiences and choosing to learn. Your thinking has changed, you are a little more patient, a little less frustrated about things that are out of your control. You may not be perfect, but you are making progress, you are gaining ground on your ability to be more and do more and that is something to be proud of. Look at yourself you are becoming more of who you want to be and that is amazing.

MY DAILY WOW AFFIRMATION

I am excited about the person I will become
My progress excites me
I am acquiring more skills
I am becoming better at what I do
I am living a full life

DAY 41

Persist until you succeed

. . .

You will have to knock on a few doors before a door is opened up to you. You may even have to knock on the same door continuously until it opens. But take heart, it will open, and if you search you will find what you are looking for. Searching requires for you to be intentional about what it is that you are looking for. It means looking with purpose and anything you do with purpose, will be fulfilled. Continue to ask and in asking be specific, it's not a generic response that you want, so ask with knowledge of the response you require. Do not ask passively or with doubt, be bold but graceful, knowing that what you want will be yours. What you so desire will be yours, you just have to believe and be active in getting it, don't stop and remain persistent.

MY DAILY WOW AFFIRMATION

I will continue to persist
I will not stop until my dreams are realised
I will continue to strive to achieve my goals
I will do whatever it takes to be successful
I am hopeful and intentional regarding my goals

DAY 42

Use your past to motivate you

. . .

The past can remind you of your failures, or times when you didn't do so well, mistakes you made, or regrets you have. However the past doesn't have to be such a negative experience reliving an incident you would rather forget. Rather the past can be used as a way to measure the extent of your improvement and how far you want to go. There was a time when even the most elementary things appeared difficult to you, but with time and practice you made improvements. These same principles can be applied in future endeavours, what do you find hard to do that you will like to master in the future? Use your past successes as motivation that it can be done and that you will be able to do it. It will involve practice, maybe a little discipline and focus but you will achieve it if you stick with it.

MY DAILY WOW AFFIRMATION

I am motivated by my past
I use my past lessons to guide my steps
I am motivated to succeed
I am not where I used to be and that excites me
I am disciplined

DAY 43

Every sacrifice brings you closer to your destination

. . .

There is a price to pay for anything worth having in life and the most costly things come with some sort of sacrifice. The price you pay may require you letting go of some things, giving more of yourself, working harder, putting in more effort and time. To obtain something you have never had before, you will have to do things that, you may have never done before. The more you sacrifice the closer you get to where you want to be, the more effort you put in, the more results you see. To achieve something you have set out to do is invaluable, because what you gain is not always quantifiable. The sacrifice is always more than what you actually do, you can't put a value on it, but it is always worth it in the end.

MY DAILY WOW AFFIRMATION

My sacrifices are worth it
I am closer to my goals
I turn my pain into gain
I have self-discipline
I will endure for the greater good

DAY 44

Don't give up

. . .

If I could scream this from the highest mountain top so it would resound constantly in your ears, I would. I know it's hard. I know it's lonely. I know it's long. I know it's a sacrifice. I know you are tired and have absolutely nothing left. I know you have been running on empty and you are weak all over. I know, I understand, I have been there. But I promise you with everything within me, everything you are going through is temporary! It has an expiry date. Don't completely throw in the towel. What you are going through is building you up for better things. It is refining your character, it is strengthening your mind, the rewards far supersede the struggle. You are not just doing it for yourself but for generations to come who will hear your story and have hope.

MY DAILY WOW AFFIRMATION

I will not give up
I am not a quitter
I see things through to the end
I will compete all I need to do
I have no doubt in my ability

DAY 45

There is freedom in being unique

. . .

It's common for you to want to go unnoticed, blend into the crowd and be "normal". But the most normal thing is actually what sets you apart. Your differences and the very thing that makes you unique, is common in everyone. But it is also a distinctive gift, it liberates you from a mould that society may want you to fit into, a system that limits your creativity and growth. Your very make up and formation is created from something that is matchless. It is your unique print in the universe to let everyone know you were here. Your DNA, forms the basis of who you are, shaped by your ancestry and partly your environment. Take time to refine your skills, nurture your passions and discover what makes you happy. Don't put pressure on yourself to be something other than who you already are. Enjoy the freedom of being you.

MY DAILY WOW AFFIRMATION

My uniqueness liberates me
I am one of a kind
I am special
I am set apart
I am in a league of my own

DAY 46

Stay around people that reflect who you want to be and how you want to feel, that force is powerful

. . .

It is crucial in life not just to have a physical cleanse or detox, but you have to do a people cleanse also. It is vital that you get rid of all the toxic and negative energies in your life. Do an honest evaluation of your relationships and if necessary, do a complete clear out of the company you keep, especially if that company is weighing you down, draining you or robbing you of your peace. Cling to those people who uplift you, encourage you, who build you up and make you strong. Look to your role models, close and far. Listen to their words of advice. Attach yourself to friends who are walking in the same direction as you. You are a stronger force when you walk the path together.

MY DAILY WOW AFFIRMATION

I welcome great people into my life
I cut myself off from bad energy
My networks are getting better
The right people will come into my life
The right people will find me

DAY 47

You have to be willing to fail in order to win

. . .

Failure isn't final, in fact the more you are willing to fail, is the more you are likely to succeed! It is through failure, that you learn how not to do things. It is a teacher and guide. Use your failures as stepping stones that you climb to reach new heights. Failure is a reality check, it centres you, it's experiencing the worst, so you don't have to be afraid of what getting it wrong feels and looks like.

Failure is a temporal incident and moment in time, it will soon be forgotten. However, the rewards of success are long lasting. I'm sure you fell a countless amount of times when you attempted to walk for the first time, but you didn't let it bother you because you knew eventually you would get it.

You will eventually win the war even if you lose today's battle. Keep failing until you win.

MY DAILY WOW AFFIRMATION

I will not be phased by failure
I will win even if at first I fail
In the end I win
My wins are permanent
I will keep winning

DAY 48

Progression over Perfection

. . .

Every step is better than no steps, movement forward is better than staying stationary. It can take time, but time will pass. What is key, is what you do in that time. With time, progression becomes perfection through practice. Keep improving, keep learning and keep refining your skills. Soon those little steps will be huge milestones. The pace at which you go is irrelevant, so do not compare your journey with anyone else, run your own race, stay in your own lane, focus on your journey. Don't go off track, trying to keep up with what is going on around you, those are mere distractions which will slow you down. Move at a rate where you won't lack zeal or burn out later on in the course. Take pride in every step knowing that it is bringing you closer to where you want to be, you are gaining ground through your progress.

MY DAILY WOW AFFIRMATION

I am progressing
I am moving forward
I am getting the job done
I am improving with practice
Each step takes me closer to my goal

DAY 49

If it matters to you, you will find a way, if it does not you will find an excuse

. . .

Be a solution finder, a problem solver, a way maker. Do not always find a reason why it won't work, or why it seems impossible. Stop finding excuses and reasons to talk yourself out of an opportunity because on the surface it appears difficult. It may be hard, but you can do it, you are strong enough, smart enough and wise enough. You have what it takes to conquer this challenge, and even if you feel like you don't, you can find a way to beat it by being creative or seeking help. What you may require is a bit of motivation. So, find a reason why you need to overcome this hurdle. Make it important and personal, then look beyond yourself at the other people that will benefit from your persistence and success. Now you have a reason to win and not an excuse for losing.

MY DAILY WOW AFFIRMATION

I will always find a way
I find solutions to problems
I am a problem solver
I am smart
I have no excuses

DAY 50

You are more stronger than you think

. . .

Stop counting yourself out before you have even given it a chance. You can fall a thousand times, but get up one thousand and one. You are not weak because you fall but rather you are strong because you are determined not to stay down. Every time you get back up, you are building muscle. Every time you try again, you are getting closer. You have more in you still. You are resilient, you are determined. You don't cave under pressure, instead you rise to the challenge, you stand in adversity. And if you have never done so before. Now is the time to be brave, stand strong and fight, for you are much stronger than you can imagine. You just needed the opportunity to show strength and use your muscle.

MY DAILY WOW AFFIRMATION

I am strong
I am confident
I am bold
I am not fazed by challenges
I will not give up

DAY 51

You owe it to yourself to be patient with yourself

· · ·

Just like Rome wasn't built in a day, neither were you. It took at least around 9 months for you to be formed in the womb before you were ready to come into this world. And it took some time for you to learn how to crawl, walk and talk. Anything that involves you learning a new skill requires time. Being frustrated with your progress will not speed up the process, in fact it could very well do the opposite. So, don't be so hard on yourself, you owe it to yourself to be patient with yourself. Understand that you will get there eventually. Once you remain committed and consistently attempt to keep on improving with practice and determination, it doesn't matter that it is not straight away. You may even take one step forward and five steps back, keep at it, progress is progress, you will get there in the end.

MY DAILY WOW AFFIRMATION

I will not put unnecessary pressure on myself
I am patient with myself
I know that good things take time
I am willing to wait for greatness
I am a work in progress

DAY 52

Discipline is a choice between what you desire now and what you desire most

. . .

It's so easy to give into the temptation of self-indulgence. Whether that be eating things we know we shouldn't or spending time or money on the things we know we ought not to. Discipline seems difficult, it can feel like pain, suffering or hardship. But this feeling is temporary, the reward however is long lasting. Don't compromise with self-indulgence because of a temporary discomfort or for a minute of pleasure. These temporary things will be forgotten, and eventually you will reap the rewards of self-control. It is important for you to remember that discipline is not innate, it is learnt. You can build discipline over time by making small adjustments to your behaviour, until it becomes a habit. By doing this you strengthen your willpower and your ability to make decisions that best serve who you want to be and where you want to go. So, choose to exercise discipline daily.

MY DAILY WOW AFFIRMATION

I have self-control
I am disciplined
I am patient
I will not give in to temptation
I have strong willpower

DAY 53

The regrets of tomorrow can be avoided by the choices of today

. . .

Stop regretting the failure of yesterday and fearing the failures of tomorrow. All you really have control over is this moment right now and the decisions you make today. Learn from your mistakes, try again without fear, have the vision in clear sight, write you plan of action, then make it happen. Be present by living in the now, and choosing to be happy now. Your emotions can sometimes be deceptive as they are easily swayed by external factors. Learn to get a greater command on your emotions by aligning them with your thoughts. You are in control of your thoughts, you can choose what you perceive and you interpret a situation to be. With this knowledge always choose thoughts of joy and peace. This can be hard at first but requires you to gradually programme your mind, so that when something happens you are not reactive. Cool, calm and composed that's you.

MY DAILY WOW AFFIRMATION

I put my plan in action
I do not live in regret
I make well thought through decisions
I am perceptive
I go for what I want

DAY 54

You are what you do daily, make excellence a habit through your daily actions

. . .

You do not become successful by accident. Greatness is acquired through habit; things that you repeatedly do over a period of time, to improve and later master. Excellence is something you continually strive for. It's something that involves going the extra mile, working a little longer, trying a little harder, pushing a little further. The little things you do today actually can make big changes in your life tomorrow. You must have the foresight to see that where you want to go and what you want to do, is possible with hard work and determination. The basis of every success story is intention, that desire and determination to win, to excel and to achieve. You have to want it and continue to work at it until you get it. And you win because you are willing to do what it takes to become a winner.

MY DAILY WOW AFFIRMATION

I am a product of my actions
I create good habits
I am building good character
I am committed to growth
I am determined to be successful

DAY 55

You have everything within you to be what you want to be

. . .

There is a liberty you feel when you discover the power of the light within yourself. This can manifest itself as self-validation instead of external acceptance. You don't need anyone to recognise your worth because you know exactly who you are. Knowing who you are reveals what's in you to become all that you can be. It releases you to walk in your full purpose. You are unashamed of shining because you know your light does not dim others and does not compete to be brighter. You just shine because you know you are fulfilling purpose, you are walking in your true form and bringing hope, dispersing darkness and revealing truth while doing so. Your light is a guide, a beacon of hope, and brings reassurance. You don't need anything outside of yourself to be you and to become more of who you are, you are self-sufficient and whole.

MY DAILY WOW AFFIRMATION

I am filled with greatness
I have everything I need
I am a light
I am fulfilling purpose
I compete with no one

DAY 56

Don't become so focused on the finish line that you forget to appreciate the journey

. . .

It's great to be focused and goal orientated, but you don't get to experience the full depth, worth and beauty of finishing when you cannot appreciate and enjoy every moment involved in getting there. Take moments to reflect on the journey, take in the moment, allow yourself to feel and be human. Take yourself off auto-pilot and experience immersion in what is happening right now. Take stock of how you feel, be in-tune with all of your senses, what does this moment in your journey mean for you?

Live in the moment not just during good times. Let your experience shape and mould you, let it leave it's mark, not as a tattoo, but as a gentle reminder of where you are coming from. Allow your experience to sharpen and refine you, and your craft. It's not just about finishing but it's about being whole and complete when you get there.

MY DAILY WOW AFFIRMATION

I am living my best life
I am enjoying the process
I choose to enjoy the journey
I am grateful for this process
I am grateful for this gift

DAY 57

What you learn and who you become in the process of waiting is even more valuable than what you waited for

. . .

Who are you becoming in pursuit of your goal? While you strive to reach your desired role or position in life how are you being shaped? Is your character being refined? Are your circles reflecting the person you want to be? Are you stronger mentally? More understanding? Humble? Wise? Kind? Caring?

If you have lost the essence of who you are and can no longer recognise yourself, check the path you are walking on to get to your final destination. If this is the route you have to take, when you get there will you even like yourself, let alone love yourself? People will come and leave your life for different reasons, but you are stuck with yourself, so do not compromise what you know is right in pursuit of status. Remain integral, so that when you get to where you are going, you can maintain your self-respect and dignity.

MY DAILY WOW AFFIRMATION

I am becoming better daily
The process is making me greater
There are lessons I'm learning in waiting
I am becoming more patient
I am becoming more of who I want to be

DAY 58

Grow through your adversity

. . .

What doesn't kill you, will surely make you stronger. You made it through another second, minute, hour, day, week, month, year. Don't miss it! The lessons to be learnt, connections to be built, the goals to strive for. A seed has to be buried and die before it can grow and bear fruit. Don't let your situation overwhelm you or overcome you. Grow through it. Let life's challenges be the nutrients to feed you from the roots, let the storms be the water you need to grow. Criticism can be likened to the scorching of the sun, instead of letting it burn you or you shrivel under its heat, let it act as light, to guide you and transform you for the better. The strongest, longest-surviving trees grow through adverse conditions. Learn from your surroundings, use it to become all that you can be.

MY DAILY WOW AFFIRMATION

I am growing
Adversity does not discourage me
Adversity reveals my strength
I am stronger than ever before
I am resilient

DAY 59

Trust your greatness

. . .

Stop doubting yourself, you are capable of more than you know. Give yourself a chance to be great. Don't rule out a successful outcome without even trying. Past failures do not have to determine future outcomes. Trust the greatness within, you are fearfully and wonderfully made and are absolutely capable of overcoming even when the odds are against you. You have success deep within you, you just need to draw it out of yourself. This may take time and patience, but if you take a chance on yourself, it will surprise you when you discover how much you can actually do. The belief that someone has in your ability is insignificant if you do not believe and trust in yourself. Take a chance on yourself and keep taking chances until you prove yourself right. Your greatness is real, it is tangible, now all you need to do is stir it up.

MY DAILY WOW AFFIRMATION

I trust the person I am becoming
I trust the process
My efforts are not wasted
I am great
I am successful

DAY 60

The love you crave is closer than you think

. . .

Self-love and acceptance is the best sort of love. If you don't truly love and value yourself, it's challenging for someone to know how to love and value you. Know how to love yourself. Part of loving yourself is forgiving yourself and believing in yourself. Do not seek validation from people outside, validate yourself. Love on your imperfections, as you are a work in progress, not a finished product. You are being moulded and formed into the person you have invested in, if that isn't very much, then you won't like the results. So, invest in yourself, learn to love and appreciate yourself and don't wait for others to do this. Put value in who you are now and the person you are becoming. You are worthy and deserving of love, especially a love much deeper than any other love. Be good to yourself, love and accept who you are and want to be.

MY DAILY WOW AFFIRMATION

I do not depend on love externally
I cherish love as a gift
I give love freely
I value the love given to me
I am worthy to be loved

DAY 61

The road may be difficult, but the destination is beautiful

. . .

The journey can get a little rough, lonely and challenging. But if you continue and do not go off course, you will be led to a rewarding gift of a beautiful destination. Don't give up, you are setting the trail ablaze so that a path is created for those who are coming up behind you.

You are overcoming the struggle for many more than just yourself. You are restoring hope for those who did not believe it could be done. It's hard now, but the glory far outweighs the current struggle. You will in time be thanked with love and warmth from those coming after you. Resist the temptation to stop or to turn back. It would have all been in vain if you do not make it to the end. The destination is worth the challenging road that leads to it. Your reward is waiting for you at the end of the journey, if you do not give up.

MY DAILY WOW AFFIRMATION

My journey is beautiful
I am not fazed by difficulty
The pain won't last
I will overcome
I will not be taken off course

DAY 62

Let go and let be

. . .

You can't be in control of everything all of the time. There will be times you are going to have to let things go and just trust that everything will work out in the end. Trust that your steps are ordered and that you are being led along a path that will ultimately take you to your goal. Even if it means taking uncertain steps, be at peace that whatever route you take it will lead you to your desired destination. Part of letting go is not having all the answers and being ok with that. Another part of letting go, is not having an expectation that you want met, which involves the actions or response of people or situations you have no control of. Whatever will be will be, whatever happens will happen. You can only act on what you have control of and it is important that you are ok with that.

MY DAILY WOW AFFIRMATION

I let go of the things outside of my control
I let go of pain
I let go of hurt
I am no longer weighed down by extra baggage
I am at peace with my destiny

DAY 63

The comeback is always stronger than the setback

. . .

Don't stay with your head buried in the mud after a major fall. Get back up, dust yourself off and fight. Fight for the victory which will definitely be yours if you do not give up. Let the fact that you haven't won stir up a desire within you to want it more than ever. Prove to yourself, that one day you will stand strong, tall and unshakeable. And that because of you, others can believe they too can win after a temporary defeat. So be resilient, be unwavering, get passionate. It is not over, you will not relent, you will keep going, you will rise, push, press on until you win. Your energy comes from your burning desire to eventually overcome this hurdle, to make it on the other side of this mountain, it comes from the excitement of eventually reaching the pinnacle you aspire to.

MY DAILY WOW AFFIRMATION

I will not be fazed by the setback
My comeback will be amazing
I am unshakeable
I am a force not to be reckoned with
I will win this fight

DAY 64

The ultimate project that you will ever work on is you

· · ·

It starts and finishes with you. Don't leave yourself out of the equation when working on your business, career, education, family or relationships. All those things can only be as good as you are. Invest in yourself, your mind, your body, your hobbies, your health and your faith. Treat yourself like royalty because that is what you are. You are the principal leader of the kingdom of your life, you rule your domain, your decisions are final.

Work on you, for you, to be the best you, you can be. Take pride in making yourself better. You are the most important project you can work on, because everything that comes from you is a result of what is already in you. Never stop working on yourself. You will not regret being a better version of yourself when you see the results of continuous personal development, self-care and love.

MY DAILY WOW AFFIRMATION

I am my most important project
I am my number one fan
I am my biggest cheerleader
I am a masterpiece
I am a worthy investment

DAY 65

Don't focus on what is behind you, focus on what lies before you

. . .

Don't constantly look back because you are not going in that direction. Don't carry your past as a burden weighing you down for the journey ahead. Focus on progress each step at a time, each day at a time. Have your goal in mind, your final destination before you and allow it to draw you towards it. When you have the end in mind, everything within you will want to get there. Looking back is a mere distraction, especially if you put your energy into analysing your previous steps or unnecessarily reflecting on scenarios that no longer matter. Meditating on what has been will not serve you in your present situation and will not propel you forward towards where you want to go. Learn from your past, momentarily reflect on your journey, but do not dwell on it. Do not stay stuck in what was, rather move towards what will be.

MY DAILY WOW AFFIRMATION

I have tunnel vision when it comes to my goals

I am strong

I am focused

I am persistent

I am determined

DAY 66

Don't put everything you have on display, let them guess and wonder how you continuously progress

. . .

There's no such thing as an overnight success. A lot of pain, sweat, tears, doubting, trip ups, falls, failures, fights and a whole lot of cussing may occur before most people "make it". Don't watch people watching you, keep doing what you have been doing in silence and give them a reason to watch. Don't always announce your next move, or even what it is that you are doing now. Let the results speak for themselves. Stay focused on getting results, rather than the attention it brings. There are some things that you need to keep to yourself and for yourself. Protect your interests, not because you are worried that anyone will hinder you but so that your focus is not deterred. And so that you don't take away from the hard work that got you there in the first place.

MY DAILY WOW AFFIRMATION

I am unassuming
I cannot be put in a box
I am creative
I am intriguing
I am fascinating

DAY 67

Build something that outlives beyond you

. . .

What will you be remembered for? What is your legacy? Your story? The print you leave on the earth so that we will know that you were here? Start by working on something that is beyond you, that stretches beyond your physical and natural reach, that transcends time and is not limited to location. This requires you thinking how what you do serves others. How does what you do make their life better? Do it, in not just what you say, but how you say it. Make impact, in not just what you do, but how you do it. Think about how you want to make someone feel your intent, your heart, a piece of you that you would like to give, just because you know it's the right thing to do. Work on leaving a legacy. Even if you are not seen, let someone know you were here by the impression you left.

MY DAILY WOW AFFIRMATION

I am building a legacy
I am excited for my future
My work will outlive me
My greatness will be impactful
I will change the world I live in for the better

DAY 68

Discover who you are and be just that

. . .

Don't conform to the mould formed from the opinions of society, family or friends. If you do not search and find yourself, you can end up feeling frustrated with life and stuck in a cycle. Explore what sets your soul on fire. What excites you? What makes you happy? What makes you laugh? What makes you sad? What do you like doing? What do absolutely detest? When you have answered these questions and maybe even a few more, look at yourself, what would you like to improve? What more can you do, to become more of what you want to be? Now commit yourself to being that, to be more of who you want to be. It is likely that this is the very person you were created to be. Break the mould. Be exactly who you were created to be and embrace wholeness in who you are.

MY DAILY WOW AFFIRMATION

I am discovering my strengths
I am owning who I am
I am an untold story
I am a work of art
I am passionate about who I am becoming

DAY 69

Be the light that drives out darkness, show the love that dispels hate

. . .

Drives out darkness with your light, destroy hate with the power of your love. This is probably one of the most difficult things to do but one of the most rewarding. Be the type of person that sees and brings the good in every situation. Be the one that adds value to what seems a worthless cause. Be the person that brings transformation to a negative situation by turning it into a positive one. For pain there is joy. Find a way to bring joy and laughter. For mistakes there are lessons, see the lesson in what looks like a disaster. For problems there are solutions, be the problem solver. Good will always triumph over evil, even if at times evil seems to have won temporally. Be encouraged that in time, good will be victorious. Be a force for good and use it as a weapon to be victorious over anything that stands against you.

MY DAILY WOW AFFIRMATION

I am a light
My light drives out darkness
My light gives hope
My love conquers hate
My light uncovers beauty

DAY 70

Work hard now your future self will reward you for it

. . .

It's tempting to kick back and relax, even when you know there is so much to do. It's common to be so overwhelmed by all you have to do, especially when you have demanded of yourself action towards an outcome that places you in a better position than you are now. Having at the back of your mind that the outcome is yet to be realised, it is easy to get comfortable in the now and not make the effort required to do what is necessary to see that outcome achieved. Every action or decision you make comes at a price and the price you choose to pay now either results in a reward or a further cost. You either are rewarded with the ability to enjoy the works of your labour or you pay by having to do even more work later. Which can also result in payments of regret.

MY DAILY WOW AFFIRMATION

I am not afraid of hard work
I work until completion
I am a good finisher
My future excites me
I work hard to make my dreams a reality

DAY 71

Stay motivated

. . .

What motivates you? Keep that in mind. That will lay a solid foundation, when things get tough along the way. When you enter the storms of life and it seems like you have to navigate from one challenge to another, think of the reason why you do what you do. And if you don't have a reason why, find one. Create a reason for doing what you do and for wanting to be where you want to be. Let your reason be something that moves you, something that is personal and stirs up emotion. Let your reason be a burning passion because it genuinely means something to you. Give your reason meaning. Once you have figured what this is, hold onto it with all your might, keep it in sight, remind yourself of it daily. Use it to stay motivated and on course to make it to the finish line.

MY DAILY WOW AFFIRMATION

I am motivated

I am committed

I am focused

I will stay encouraged

I will stay hopeful

DAY 72

If what you are doing doesn't add value, stop doing it

. . .

Why are you doing the things you do? Especially when it involves your career, hobbies, maintaining certain relationships etc. What are you doing? Do you add value? And even more importantly does it add value to you? Doing something charitable, although it may come at a cost or sacrifice of your time, your self-worth and pride is elevated by your selfless service, which becomes part of the mark you leave in the hearts of the people you help. But if you are in a career think about who you are becoming, is it adding to your self-worth? How about certain relationships, habits and hobbies? If they don't add to your health, wealth and growth, either mentally, spiritually or physically, it is likely that it is subtracting from you and you are depreciating each time you continue. Don't let anything rob you of your value or worth.

MY DAILY WOW AFFIRMATION

I will not waste time
I will be mindful of where I use my energy
I will add value in all I do
I will invest in worthy causes
My value is important

DAY 73

If not now, then when

. . .

You can only put off certain things in your life for so long, if you want it to happen, you have to take action now. Apply for that job. Change career. Start that business. Go for that audition. Buy that house or apartment. Go on that course. Do that training. Go for that promotion. Make that relocation. Go on that holiday. Ask that guy or lady out. Propose to the love of your life. Ask that question. Get the help you need. Take that once in a lifetime opportunity. Write that book, or song. Build that school. Start that campaign. Start that diet. Start that fitness plan. Lose the excess weight. Quit smoking, drinking and harming yourself. Whatever you do, don't procrastinate or delay. Stop letting the idea circulate in your mind and remain as just a hopeless dream. Give it life, plan for success and believe you can do it.

MY DAILY WOW AFFIRMATION

I will take action now
I will make continuous action towards my goals
I will get the job done
I am effective and efficient
I start and finish well

DAY 74

Purpose is birthed when your passion, your mission, your vision and profession meet

. . .

Often it can be hard to define purpose or to even find it. If you are struggling to get clarity about something that you really like, or that makes you feel inward peace and joy. What is your ideal profession? What would you like to do in your lifetime? It doesn't have to even be something that exists right now. You may desire to create or design something completely new to make life easier or better for people, or that is really important to you. Fulfil your purpose by finding out what you love, what you are great at and can add some profitable value to you. something that the world is in need of, even if the world only means one person.

You may discover this lies in your passions, profession or even a hobby. Live for more than yourself, live to fulfil purpose and enjoy life while doing it.

MY DAILY WOW AFFIRMATION

I am passionate about my vision
I am fulfilling purpose
My vision excites me
My purpose drives my decisions
I am working on fulfilling purpose

DAY 75

Delay is not denial

. . .

Don't feel like you are being side-lined, rejected, put-out, missed-out, overlooked, left behind, disregarded or slept-on. Everyone and everything has it's time. Delay comes when an expectation is not met, delay is not definitive, don't get discouraged, keep your hope burning. In fact, you will often find that although your initial expectations felt like they were not met, what you need will come right on time. And if it hasn't come yet, it isn't time. You still need to prepare and get ready for it to come and for it to happen. Whilst waiting, do not think the grass is greener on the other side, it is greener where it is looked after. Keep looking after yourself and preparing for what is to come. So that when your time comes, you are ready for it and can manage this new level of responsibility to your full capacity, enjoying every moment.

MY DAILY WOW AFFIRMATION

I am favoured
Great opportunities will be available to me
The wait will be worth it
I will not be discouraged by the delay
I am expectant of good news

DAY 76

Never underestimate the power of your prayers and a good plan

. . .

What is it that you really want? There is power in what you say. What you find in life is that a lot of what you say shapes the life you are living. So, if there is something you want out of life, say it, believe it, and plan for it. Act like it has already happened and almost like magic you see things begin to align themselves to what you have demanded out of life. It's like when you want to buy a car, you start seeing that same make and model everywhere. What you find is when you demand from life a particular desire that you have, you become more aware of the opportunities that you need to make it possible. For some reason doors that seemed close, start to open, people that can be of help start showing up, your confidence rises. So, act out in faith, pray and plan.

MY DAILY WOW AFFIRMATION

My prayers are being answered
I am preparing for wins
I do not underestimate my skill
I know my diligence will pay off
The right doors are opening for me

DAY 77

Be fearless

. . .

What are you afraid of? Is it factual? Is it final? What you may find is that a lot of what you fear has not happened and it is likely that it will never happen. It is a fictional, false scenario that you have started preparing for and expecting with no actual evidence. Even if the worse happens, you will get through it, you will survive. Instead of planning and expecting the worse, prepare and plan for a positive outcome. Yes, things can go terribly wrong, but they can also go fantastically well. Plan for things to go well. Be fearless, even if the worse happens, you will cope. It can be fixed. You can learn something and make corrective steps towards a better outcome. Do not let fear cripple or stop your progress. Things can turn in your favour, great things can happen for you, the result can lead to your good fortune.

MY DAILY WOW AFFIRMATION

I am not afraid
I am bold
I am confident
I am secure in my ability
I am confident the outcome will be in my favour

DAY 78

In less than three months, you will thank yourself for starting

. . .

When you do something repeatedly over time, it becomes a habit. A habit overtime shapes and forms your character. So, everything you are now is because of daily or regular choices you have repetitively made. This means you can either change for the better or worse depending on what you commit to. If you commit to being consistent in forming good habits that you have built over time, you will reap the results by the person you become. You can also improve who you are now by making choices and decisions that serve you and the person you want to become. To get there you need to make a start that will act as a foundation you can build on constantly. Eventually you will be able to say, 'I'm glad I did it' rather than 'I wish I did it'

MY DAILY WOW AFFIRMATION

I am progressing
I will reach my goals
I choose to not give up
I will commit to my development

DAY 79

If you question the power within, you give fuel to your unbelief

. . .

Stay positive and don't give power to doubt or unbelief. It may have not been done before but what you want to happen, can happen. It is possible, you just have to believe it. Believe you are that one chance in a billion. The odds are not against you, in fact they are in your favour. You will succeed. You are that anomaly, that rare chance. Anomaly's happen all the time. It can and will totally happen for you, plan and prepare for it, but even if you don't, there is something in you, that mustard seed faith that moves mountains. Fuel your faith, because that is what will take you there. Remember all you are doing is fulfilling purpose, by expressing yourself in fullness. Don't even give doubt a look in. There is no room for doubt and faith. So, fill every part of you with all the faith you have.

MY DAILY WOW AFFIRMATION

I am powerful
I have charge over my life
I will not fuel unbelief
I speak in faith
I act in faith

DAY 80

Accept people for who they are and reject some for who they are also

. . .

Some people are in your life for a reason or a season. Make sure it's a good reason and it's in the right season. Don't take it personally when people remove themselves from your life. Where you are now and where you are going requires different connections and environments. Your circles have to shift to accommodate the person you are becoming. You have to learn to get comfortable with change, because it's to make you stronger. This can be a test of character and also to determine if you are ready to go to the next level of growth and responsibility. It is not always easy, but it is required. Some people will come back when they have been through their own process, but for now focus on yourself, because you can only be as effective as the investment you make in yourself.

MY DAILY WOW AFFIRMATION

I welcome good people into my life
I remove myself from harmful people
I distance myself from bad people
I attract people that are genuine
I attract blessed people into my life

DAY 81

Your value doesn't decrease based on someone's inability to see your worth

. . .

Your worth is indescribable. If someone can't see that, they don't need to be around you or use up your time because it will lead to a lot of wasted energy. Your worth is not determined by recognition from people. You are who you are and what you are, your value cannot be measured. You are amazing and rare. You are a masterpiece, created intelligently and specifically for a unique purpose. Know and understand this, so that you can express yourself in your entirety without holding back. The world has need of your gift. Your light is needed to illuminate the darkness. Your fire is needed to bring warmth, your wisdom is needed to solve problems. Your voice is needed to bring answers. You are necessary, you are needed, you mean something. Don't hide yourself because someone doesn't see all this in you.

MY DAILY WOW AFFIRMATION

I am worthy
I am valuable
My worth is not measured by how I am treated
My value is constantly increasing
I am precious

DAY 82

No one is you and that is your super power

. . .

Your power is in your DNA. Even if it has been done 100 times before, if it wasn't done by you it's totally brand new when you do it. Stop thinking that the market is saturated. When you do it and add your authenticity to what you do, it becomes new. And the reason why that area is saturated is because it works, people are finding success in it. There are diverse angles, groups and approaches that have not been explored, that you can invest your energy in. What do people want? You may have the answer to their needs. Focus on making whatever you produce, good quality and authentic. Stay true to yourself and give it your best. Don't short change people and don't short change yourself, don't do a half job. Don't try to be another version of somebody else. God knew what he was doing when you were created.

MY DAILY WOW AFFIRMATION

I am authentic
I am true to myself
I do not seek to be like anyone else
I am confident in myself
I am the me I need to be

DAY 83

There is no need to rush, what is meant for you will always arrive right on time

. . .

As commonly stated, 'time waits for no man', which can be very true, but you also cannot rush the hand of time. Be patient, stay focused and prepare for what is yours because it will not pass you by. It will find you, in the right place, at the right time. Work on yourself, prepare for what it is that you want, like you already know it is going to happen. While you wait be grateful for the opportunity to be used for a greater purpose. Think about the impact you will have in this new place of responsibility and how you can use it to enhance the lives of people around you. You can be used to bring value to many lives. Think about how you can use your gifts and resources, don't just dwell on what you will be receiving, the position is a gift in itself.

MY DAILY WOW AFFIRMATION

I will not rush the process
I will wait for my blessings
I will not miss out on what is for me
I am attracting everything that is meant for me
What belongs to me will find me

DAY 84

Sometimes you win, sometimes you learn

. . .

Until you win you learn. It's not over until you win. If you haven't won then there's still some way to go, keep learning, keep growing and keep rising. Everything that appears to be a loss is an opportunity to learn. What was the lesson? What can you improve in yourself so that your next attempt yields more successful results? Do you just need to keep trying? You are destined to win eventually, so with that in mind, keep trying until that happens. Be a master student, ask the right questions and deduce the answers by studying the information you have. You will eventually have your eureka moment. The answer is there, you just have to keep on looking for it. Don't relent, don't give up, it will only slow down the process. If you need to, look outside of yourself and get the help you need. Let your focus be to win at the end.

MY DAILY WOW AFFIRMATION

I am constantly learning
I learn from my wins
I learn from my losses
I am constantly improving
I am devoted to becoming better

DAY 85

Use your voice to speak life

. . .

You create the world around you with the words you speak. Use your God-given abilities to build and create the world you want to live in. Everything that exists started with a thought, then those thoughts were formed into words, which led to action. Who you are today is shaped by a thought process that you agreed to with your words. You are constantly sculpting who you are and want to be in life through what you say. To change the narrative, change what you are confessing. Use your words sparingly and with intent. Give authority to what you say by following through with actions. Be integral. Be trustworthy. Let your word be your bond. When you are undecided mentally, it shows in your conversation and in your actions, often through instability. So, say what you mean and mean what you say.

MY DAILY WOW AFFIRMATION

My voice is a tool for substance
I honour my voice
I use my words to speak life
My voice is a gift
My voice is a blessing

DAY 86

Let go of energy that is not supportive of your growth

. . .

From time to time you have to be real and look at your life to analyse your relationships. Who is bringing value and who is robbing you of your energy or God given power to fulfil your assignment?

There are people that you are going to have to love and like from a distance, because they are not refining the person you want to be. Check to see that you are not becoming inefficient and ineffective. The honest truth is that not everyone around you is necessarily for you. They do not support your progress and it's nothing personal, it just is what it is. Don't let people that try to dim your light or bring you down, get to you. Simply remove yourself from their grasp, protect your energy, as your energy and self-belief is what is needed to get you to where you are going.

MY DAILY WOW AFFIRMATION

I surround myself with the right energy
My energy is conducive for my growth
I cut myself off from energy suckers
I use my energy to progress
I am protective of my energy

DAY 87

Don't beg, force or follow. Instead, pray, work hard and be patient

. . .

Be so focused on the person you want to be in this world and the impact you want to make, that you don't have time for all the other things that will crowd your vision. Remember that is all just stuff that will get dealt with as and when appropriate. Don't get bogged down by the detail, everything will take shape as you focus in on the end result. The right doors will open, the right people will show up to help you, the opportunities that you need will present themselves and you will get the answers you are looking for. Stay prayed up, grinding and keep your faith strong, you will achieve more than you ever expected, without having to compromise your value or substance. Stay authentic and be able to reject anything that doesn't help you to fulfil the person that you are becoming.

MY DAILY WOW AFFIRMATION

Everything that is for me will find me
I will not force my blessings
My blessings will find me
My faith will attract favour
I will find the keys that open the right doors

DAY 88

Make the choice in your mind and follow it with action

. . .

All your dreams, hopes and ambitions are merely that without action. You will be required to step out of your comfort zone and take that leap of faith. Don't hesitate, just do it. Don't let your feelings overwhelm you. You may have momentary fear or anxiety because what you are trying to accomplish takes you out of your comfort zone, but I promise you that when you take action you will see results. To see effective results, be intentional about the actions that you take. Think about the results you want and what you will have to do to get those results, then work backwards. If you do not know what actions are required, then all you can do is try and learn. Remember every attempt brings you closer to the results you want. You are learning, becoming a master and teacher for people coming up behind you.

MY DAILY WOW AFFIRMATION

I turn my plans into actions
My choices are aligned to my purpose
I act on my faith
I am intentional about the actions I take
I strive for good results

DAY 89

You have to win in your mind before you can win in your life

. . .

Winners usually win before they've actually won. They have predicted the outcome by committing themselves to do whatever it takes to win. They have the prize fixed in their mind.. Now it may not be a conscious thing, but something within them is determined to do what is needed to win. They give and do their best. What do you really want out of life? You may or may not know the specifics, but in order to win, you have to know in your mind that you have already won. You have to make up in your mind that those passions, dreams and visions are already going to happen. You have to know and believe the actions you are taking will lead to the results that you want. You have to be willing to do what is required to see it through, first in your mind and then in your actions.

MY DAILY WOW AFFIRMATION

I fix my attention on winning
I programme my mind for accomplishment
I fuel my mind for success
My mind serves me and works with me
My mind is focused

DAY 90

You are far stronger than a diamond, they can never break you

. . .

Bend if you have to, but do not let anything or anyone break you. Do not bow, do not succumb, you are stronger than you can ever imagine. And even if you feel like your strength is failing, a strength within that comes from a source greater than you will rise up within you. God's strength is made perfect in your weakness and whether you ask for it or not, if you connect to that source, it will work for you. You are greater than every trial, test and struggle you ever went through. Designed with intent to fulfil purpose. Stop entertaining thoughts that make you feel like less than what you are. You are all you are and more. You have great potential, you do not know what you will be, but it already exists within you before you become it. Therefore, stand in your strength with confidence.

MY DAILY WOW AFFIRMATION

I am more precious than a diamond
I am a formidable force
I am unbreakable
I am strong
I can endure the pressure

DAY 91

What you struggle with today is developing the strength you need for tomorrow

. . .

Test and trials don't last always. It's building the power you need for tomorrow. Therefore, embrace the struggle today, thinking about the triumph that will be revealed when you overcome. You will overcome, you will get over this hurdle, you will win this battle. What seems like a struggle will be a stepping stone to you achieving great things. Cultivate habits that will work for you beyond today. That discipline that seems like such a gruesome task is transforming your character. It is enabling you to withstand other tasks similar to this in the future. Stick with it. Do not stop and do not give up. You can and you will conquer this challenge. Conditioning your mind and body so that going the extra mile is common practice for you. Your test is developing you for first place status every time.

MY DAILY WOW AFFIRMATION

I can withstand the storm
I can handle the challenge
I will persevere
I am becoming stronger
I am triumphant

DAY 92

You will get through this

. . .

You have the power to predict the future. In fact, you have more influence over your future than you could ever imagine. The doors you want to walk through, the platforms you want to be on, and the people you want to work with are all within your reach. Your limitations do not dictate where you will be. Your current situation is not your final destination. If you can see beyond where you are now, you can surely get there. You will get through this stage of life, this test that you are going through. Believe that you can get to where you want to be. Believe that it is closer than you think. Start to say it verbally and take steps towards where you see yourself tomorrow. Adopt an optimistic outlook. Be positive even in the midst of negativity, as that is your way out of it.

MY DAILY WOW AFFIRMATION

I will overcome
I will win this battle
I will not stop fighting until I win
I am victorious
I can do this

DAY 93

The strongest people may not always win straight away, but they don't give up when they lose

. . .

No matter what happens don't give up. Your strength is not tested by your wins, your strength is tested by your consistency. Can you be trusted with the task at hand, to see it through until the end? Will you withstand the temptation to throw in the towel when things get tough? Will you lack motivation and stop? Losing is inevitable when you give up. But losing is temporal when you refuse to give up. When you continue despite the odds stacked against you, your weakness will melt, and strength will emerge as you press on. Let your might be displayed in your persistence. Be in pursuit of turning that loss into a win. Be relentless, unyielding and unapologetic about who you are. You are deserving, you are strong, and you are a fighter.

MY DAILY WOW AFFIRMATION

I am determined to win
I will not give up
I will not be fazed by blocks in the road
I will complete my journey
In the end I win

DAY 94

When there's nothing to say, say nothing

. . .

Your actions will always speak volumes in comparison to what you say, especially when there is nothing to be said. Do not speak for the sake of it as you will be judged for everything that comes out of your mouth. Observe what is being perceived from what has already been said. What is the impact of your words? Do not reveal all in what is said. Let your words be rare and powerful. Let them be weighty and refine how you deliver them. Speak with conviction. Mean what you say and say what you mean. It's not always about having the right words to say, it's just about being present. It's not always about defending yourself, it's allowing the truth to speak for itself. It's not always about telling the world your plans, it's about allowing them to see with their own eyes once you have accomplished them.

MY DAILY WOW AFFIRMATION

I use my words wisely
I use my words to empower
I use my words to uplift
I speak life
My words are precious

DAY 95

You didn't come this far to stop now

. . .

There's still a way to go, don't give up or give in until you get there. Your friends and family are rooting for you to succeed and your enemies are waiting for your downfall. Do the right ones proud. Go all the way. Do it for yourself. To prove to yourself that you have everything in you to do what you need to do to get to where you want to go. You can accomplish what lies ahead. Even though it seems so far away and so out of your grasp now, if you continue, you will get there. There's no turning back now, you've come too far to back step, you've come too far not to get the reward for all the hard work you have put in. Keep going. You will get there. You will win. You will achieve more than you ever could imagine. Make the decision to finish the race, to run, walk, crawl if you have to, as long as you do not stop. Your prize is waiting for you at the finish line.

MY DAILY WOW AFFIRMATION

There is greatness ahead of me
Remarkable things await me
I still have wonderful things to achieve
My destiny is exceptional
The reward will be worth all I have been through

DAY 96

The real battle is in the mind

. . .

Transform your mind by educating yourself about things that impacts your social, economic, spiritual, physical and emotional wellbeing. Once your mind changes the rest will be relatively easy. If you struggle to comprehend better for yourself, it will be difficult to achieve it. You can't fight for the best externally when internally you still struggle to see yourself worthy of the best. You have to overcome in your mind. What is hindering you? Get to the root. What was said? What experience did you have that warped your mind into this state of self-doubt? Dissociate yourself from a can't mentally, look at what remains in the present, what can you do? What steps can you take? What improvements can you make? So what if you don't succeed straightaway, it is not the end. It is not over for you. You can still do something, you can still make it.

MY DAILY WOW AFFIRMATION

I have a strong mind
I will overcome every battle
I am resilient
I will push through
I will make it over this hurdle

DAY 97

Make a decision and let that decision be to win

. . .

It is within your capacity to win. What do you want out of life? Now be honest with yourself. It will require work and effort. But what will the cost of doing nothing be? And can you afford the price of not doing what it takes to fulfil your dreams? Will you be fulfilled in simply being mediocre? Will you be satisfied with not taking a chance on what could be a huge success? Or will you live in regret, feeling stuck because you didn't even try? You have to decide if it is worth it. And how much it is worth to you or the ones that are depending on you. Whatever it costs it cannot compare to what winning will be like. Winning is priceless, it keeps paying, because along the journey you are gifted with traits that will continue working for you even after you win.

MY DAILY WOW AFFIRMATION

I will do what it takes to win
I will not settle for mediocrity
I will be the best
I will make decisions that serve my purpose
I will strive for excellence

DAY 98

If you can see it, you can be it, if you can believe it, you can achieve it

. . .

When you see it in your mind, when that mental picture is clear and vivid, it's attainment is more compelling. As you demand of yourself what is needed to establish this picture, your faith rises, and the possibilities are amplified in your favour. As your belief grows, you are able to formulate its conception, nurture and cultivate it, until it becomes reality. The work involved is no longer strenuous because you see the end goal. You are no longer fearful of the fight because all you see is the victory. The price is reasonable because you know you will be paid in full with profit. Don't overlook the importance of your sight, your vision depends on it. Anything that wants to blur your vision will act as a hindrance to you. Your vision of the future is your proof that it can be done, so make it real.

MY DAILY WOW AFFIRMATION

I see greatness ahead of me
I know I will fulfil my vision
I am confident in my destination
I believe in my future
I will achieve my goals

DAY 99

Stay focused

. . .

There are so many things in your life that can distract you. These things can take you off course, slow you down or stop you completely. Don't let this happen. Always have your goal at the forefront of your mind. Do not entertain distractions, stay focused. Think about how good it will feel to complete what lies ahead. More often than not distractions are untimely, it's not that you shouldn't at all, it's just that you shouldn't right now. If what you are doing does not bring you closer to where you are going or help you to become the person you want to be, you have to be honest with yourself and operate in self-control. Don't tempt yourself, although you are strong, know what your weakness is and don't feed it. Let your discipline be your fuel to be better and do better.

MY DAILY WOW AFFIRMATION

I am focused
I do not get distracted
I stay on track
I keep account of where I am going
I have self-control

DAY 100

Your unique gifts will bring you before the right people

. . .

Do you have the ability to make things better than they are? Can you create something from nothing? Can you make people feel better than they felt before? These abilities are skills that are special gifts assigned to you to fulfil your purpose. Nurture your skill. Make it your own. Refine it so that it serves those around you. And as you do this it will put you before people that can change your life for the better. Seek to bring value to everyone that comes into contact with you, through your skill. Let them feel like their life has improved because they experienced something you did. That is how you make your life have meaning. People are drawn to you because your ability is a light that brings hope. Your light attracts people because it gives reassurance and joy all through you just being yourself.

MY DAILY WOW AFFIRMATION

My gift is making room for me
My creativity is opening doors for me
I will meet the right people
I am connecting with destiny enablers
Spaces in high places are being created for me

DAY 101

You will be honoured for your diligence

. . .

Things will work out for you through your persistence and willingness to continue despite whether you see results straight away or not,. You will be rewarded for not giving up. Expect great and wonderful things to happen. Feel and extract positivity from your surroundings and all you desire will come to you. When you change your thinking your whole world changes, doors begin to fly open. As you expect great things, you attract them from every situation and environment. You are drawn to what you desire and what you desire is drawn to you as you continue to thrive for its realisation. Work hard on yourself, motivate yourself, do not be dependent on encouragement from external sources only. Let your passion come from within, fuel it with your belief of what you hope will be, trusting that you do not believe in vain.

MY DAILY WOW AFFIRMATION

I am being rewarded for my diligence
I will no longer be overlooked
Favour will find me
I will receive many accolades
I will be widely celebrated

DAY 102

Clothe yourself in confidence

. . .

Clothing is there to cover us, protect us and to allow us to express ourselves as well as for other purposes. Likewise let confidence cover you, protect you from negativity and express your belief in your unique ability. Your confidence will attract remarkable opportunities that you only could have imagined. When you lack confidence, it is not that you do not have the skill or ability, it is that your perception of your ability is skewed. You actually have no idea what you can or cannot do, especially when you haven't done it before. And only because you failed at your first few attempts it does not mean you won't ace it on your next attempt. Don't let anything knock your confidence, it's like stepping out naked, you wouldn't really want to be that vulnerable or exposed like that ordinarily, so clothe yourself in confidence.

MY DAILY WOW AFFIRMATION

I wear confidence
I exude joy
I carry peace
I am crowned with honour
I walk in faith

DAY 103

Dream Big

. . .

Let your dreams, hopes and vision expand beyond you, let it transcend time, location, backgrounds and cultures, let its impact be universal. That's a dream worth having and worth working on. It is a dream that may seem overwhelming initially, but it is also a compelling one. Do something that will leave a legacy after you, that will live beyond you. What does this dream look like if you took all this into consideration? If your dream could expand and have no limits, where would it go? Who would it reach? How would it get there? Make your dream detailed and creative. As you think up a gripping story in which the course of your life could take shape. Imagine the possibilities if this dream was to come true. Imagine what you could do and who you could help. What appears like a dream is so possible, keep believing and dreaming.

MY DAILY WOW AFFIRMATION

My dreams excite me
I am not intimidated by my goals
I am not overwhelmed by my vision
I know the path has been made clear for me
I am confident I will reach my destination

DAY 104

Be patient, the best things happen unexpectedly

. . .

Keep going, even if you feel like your efforts are not making any difference. Be consistent even when you cannot see any results, the reward itself is being achieved regardless as you are learning to be disciplined. Continue, the results will come and just like that, once it starts it will flow, and will not stop, everything you desire will come at once and it won't end. Prepare for abundance, for more than what you can expect. Will you be able to contain everything that is about to come your way? You can't get prepared when you need to be prepared. So, while you are waiting, prepare, get ready for all you hope to happen and more. What do you need to specifically do for what you are expecting? Do just that. Don't get impatient or complacent, stay focused and equipped for what is about to come your way.

MY DAILY WOW AFFIRMATION

Great things await me
Better is coming
Good things are on the way
I am expectant of my dreams being fulfilled
I am hopeful that things are working out for me

DAY 105

Make it happen

. . .

If you earnestly want things to happen, you got to make them happen. Get up, stand up and show up

Opportunities come and go but it is up to you to take them when you get them. At times you will be required to even create your own opportunities, you will have to put yourself out there to get through the door. You will have to speak up to be heard. Making it happen requires you to take action. You will need to take a leap of faith, if you are not certain about the outcome act anyway. You are actively doing something because you want to see a result, you want something to change and you know it will involve you moving out of your comfort zone before you see what you want take shape. So, go ahead and do what it takes.

MY DAILY WOW AFFIRMATION

I am working on my goals
I am taking the right actions to fulfil my vision
I am taking steps forward daily
I am welcoming opportunities
I am going higher

DAY 106

Build on the foundations you have laid

. . .

Starting is good, but equally as important as the foundation, is what you build. First plan and then build. Growth is important. There is an expectation to be met, one that you demand of yourself and one that others demand of you. It is important not to let yourself down. You started because you believed in your ability to complete the task at hand. So do just that, build, step by step, brick by brick, be consistent, do not start and stop, pace yourself, keep going. You have all the tools you need inside of you to finish well. Let what you build be solid, fortified and formidable. Let it be worth the hard work you are putting in to complete it. Let it be something that you will be proud of. Let it be long-lasting and distinctive. Let it be a true reflection of who you are.

MY DAILY WOW AFFIRMATION

My foundation is solid
I am working on building myself
What I am building is long-lasting
Nothing will bring me down
I am fortified

DAY 107

Excuses don't reside here

. . .

Do not entertain excuses, you are a doer, you are not someone that gives reasons to back down or back out of what you know you are meant to be doing. You do not find excuses as to why you should not, but you find reasons as to why you should. Whatever you want to do, whatever level you want to go to next, you cannot have excuses. Find a way and if one cannot be found make a way. People that have excuses do not go very far, they frequently regress. But that is not you, you are about progression and growth. Be active, make action a habit, take chances and risks, so you become familiar and comfortable with uncertainty. In doing this, don't ever talk yourself out of an opportunity, you can do everything, you are bold, confident and strong.
If anyone can do it, it is you.

MY DAILY WOW AFFIRMATION

I am not moved by excuses
I am motivated by action
I do not find excuses for failure
I find reasons to succeed
I always find a way to get to where I am going

DAY 108

Invest in yourself

. . .

You are your biggest most important investor. Take a risk on yourself, all or nothing. You, won't let you, down. The return is great and will continue to appreciate with time. Everything you put in yourself will yield a great return. Put the work in, it is not in vain. Put the time in, it is not being wasted. You are storing riches as you develop yourself. You are building wealth as you take charge of your life. And the further you go and the more you require, keep investing. As you reap, invest more so you can grow more. There, is no limit to how much you can become and attain when you keep pouring into yourself. Keep on putting the work in until all the growth outpours into the lives of those around you, until the return is so great it brings increase to anyone connected to you.

MY DAILY WOW AFFIRMATION

I am my biggest investment
I am a worthy investment
I am valuable
I am important
I am full of wealth

DAY 109

Have faith in yourself

. . .

There are many people that can let you down, but don't let yourself down. You need you to survive, literally. Your mind, your will power, your faith in yourself is everything you need to get you through. If the whole world abandons you and counts you out. Believe in yourself. You can prove everyone wrong about you. Even if momentarily you doubt your ability to improve or change, do not entertain that thought for too long, because it is not true. You absolutely can and you will do anything you set your mind to do. Know this and be confident in this belief, it is true and valid, because in believing it you give life to it. What you believe can happen and will happen, it can be done, and it will be done by you. Let your faith in yourself be supported by action. For the doubters let your actions prove them wrong and you right.

MY DAILY WOW AFFIRMATION

I believe in myself
I have faith in what I will achieve
I am capable of amazing things
I am skilled
I am competent

DAY 110

When you let your light shine it attracts success

· · ·

Your gift will always make room for you, it prepares the way for you. It is what illuminates you from the inside out. When you allow your light to shine. It brings, joy and hope. People are drawn to you. You attract success and great opportunities. Don't be afraid to shine your light, it exposes you and brings you attention, but you were built to handle everything that comes with your gift. It is not too much for you to handle. Tune in to your inner strength and power, don't be overwhelmed or let the external control you. You are in control, as your gift comes from you, it is not owned by anyone but you. Take ownership of yourself, do not let anyone manipulate or try to abuse your gift. Use your humility as a weapon to protect you and prevent you from being forced into something you do not want.

MY DAILY WOW AFFIRMATION

I am attracting success
I am worthy of every blessing that is coming my way
My gift will get me noticed
I will shine my light
I have all the strength I need

DAY 111

The greatest things emerge from adversity

. . .

Do not be afraid to embrace the struggle, it is sharpening your ability and enabling you to withstand challenges. What arises from difficulty is strength you didn't even realise you had. Greatness does not come without a process. That process may be long, hard and even lonely. But what evolves from that hardship far outweighs the pain, sweat and sometimes tears. The pain you are going through, will not last but what will result from it, will endure the test of time. Nothing worth having comes easy, the effort invested is what brings value. The value of whatever you are going through or doing to arrive at greatness is priceless and will bring you the greatest peace and satisfaction. Keep at it, don't lose heart or get discouraged, something wonderful awaits you.

MY DAILY WOW AFFIRMATION

I am becoming more sharp
I will get through any struggle
I will withstand the storm
I will be successful
I will get to my destination

DAY 112

Don't look back when you are going forward

. . .

Constantly looking back when you are trying to move forward will inevitably slow you down. To move forward quickly, you need to focus on where you are going. It is easy to get distracted. You have to resist the temptation to relive the previous steps you have taken. Focus on the steps you are taking now and where you want those steps to lead you. Do not dwell on the past, press on, keep making headway and gaining ground. If you look back for too long, you may find yourself going in that direction, going around in a circle and although it appears like you are moving forward you are only taking the same path you have previously taken. This is both wasted time, effort and energy. You haven't come this far to go backwards.

MY DAILY WOW AFFIRMATION

I will press forward
I will push through
I will not go backwards
I am going to achieve my goals
I am closer than ever before

DAY 113

Good things take time

. . .

Anything great and worth happening does not happen overnight. A lot of effort and hard work goes into things that are supposed to last long. So do not grow weary if what you want is taking time, it is because what is being formed is good. It will set you up for greater and better things. Be patient with yourself and trust the timing of your life. Everything that is for you will happen in due time. You do not need to rush or force it. Let it take the time it needs, so it is not premature and so that you are prepared for it when it eventually comes. Most things that appear to happen overnight, took years of preparation and a lot of hard work. Wait for your turn, when it is your time, your diligence will reward you with a long lasting gift.

MY DAILY WOW AFFIRMATION

I will wait patiently
I know good things are coming
I am excited about the results
I will be rewarded for not giving up
I am trusting everything will happen in due time

DAY 114

You are filled with purpose, destiny, significance, strength and value

. . .

Everything you need is already in you. Endure your process and become all that you were created to be.

You were created to create, so get creative, fulfil purpose, relentlessly shine your light and show others how to do the same. You are important. You have significance. You matter. Things would not be the same without you. You are necessary. You are important. You are a crucial part of creation. You came at the right time and everything that has happened to you, is to make you into the person you are becoming so that you can serve and operate in the fullness of your purpose. You have a destiny and it is great. Believe in it and be confident in it. You are relevant. Live in your truth which is that you are an essential part of this universe functioning the way it does. Be confident in that truth.

MY DAILY WOW AFFIRMATION

I am significant
I am a creator of life-changing inventions
I am engineered to do awesome things
I believe in the dream
I am driven by purpose

DAY 115

Hardships transform you from ordinary to extraordinary

. . .

Ordinary people live without much change or conflict. They avoid anything that will take them away from their comfort zone. They are happy to settle rather than demand more or greater. They prefer the easy way, not exerting energy and using too much effort. They are afraid of growth and unfamiliarity. They want to keep things the same. However, if you want better and more out of life, you have to be willing to face temporary hardship. You have to allow yourself to be stretched and challenged. For expansion and a greater reach, you have to be willing to do more and put more effort in, to yield better and greater results. You cannot be averse to change as change develops you and allows you to grow. To be extraordinary, you have to go the extra mile and give more of yourself. Become comfortable with being stretched, its for your enlargement.

MY DAILY WOW AFFIRMATION

I am extraordinary
I learn from my struggles
I do not let conflict discourage me
I grow through adversity
I am a high achiever

DAY 116

There is a blessing in every lesson

. . .

Learning isn't always easy and isn't always fun, sometimes it can be very time-consuming, tiresome, boring, stressful and difficult. So why do it? Why put yourself through the agony of programming your brain with new information it is not naturally used to receiving? Why sacrifice valuable time from your already hectic schedule to facilitate knowledge or understanding some new information or practice? Why do, the same thing over and over repeatedly with the expectation it will somehow eventually stay in your mind? You rarely learn something new for the sake of just learning something new. On the contrary, you learn something new because of what you get in return, the expected outcome, reward, achievement and accomplishment at the end of it. The value is not solely in the lesson itself but what the lesson yields. So, focus on the blessing in every lesson.

MY DAILY WOW AFFIRMATION

I receive the blessings from the lesson

I am stronger

I am wiser

I am more discerning

I have more direction

DAY 117

The pain you feel now is forming the strength you need for later

. . .

Yes it does get incredibly difficult, extremely challenging and it can even be painful, but the end result is worth it all.

There is a famous quote in the bible that says 'the present suffering is not worthy to be compared to the glory that will be revealed in us'. Wow what a powerful statement!

The glory, do it for the future glory that will be revealed in you. The early mornings, the late nights, the long hours the pushing through, the pain, the tears. You are becoming stronger, wiser, more able to do things that you could not do before. The pain you once felt is now the fuel behind your strength, battles you once feared now excite you, because you know you will win and victory will be yours. So, don't focus on the pain, focus on becoming stronger and getting the glory.

MY DAILY WOW AFFIRMATION

My pain is fuel for my gain
I am getting stronger daily
Better is coming in my life
The future glory is manifesting for me
I am victorious

144

DAY 118

Design a life you enjoy living

. . .

There is no point of working so hard to make a success of your life if you do not even enjoy the person you are becoming or the life you are living. Fall in love with what you are doing and becoming every day. Enjoy your journey and process because of what it is making you do and become. Live the life that you will fall in love with daily. A life that you want to replay over and over in your head. Do this by making decisions every day that you can respect and can be proud of. Life comes with plots and twists that we never expected and there can be a happy ending if you choose to write your own script. Don't rely on anyone or anything to make you happy. Let your happiness be birthed from within. Let it be determined by an internal thermostat that you control.

MY DAILY WOW AFFIRMATION

I am living a full life
I am living a life I enjoy
I am taking control of my happiness
I will live a life I am proud of
I am grateful for my life

DAY 119

Nothing about you is mediocre

. . .

Society uses averages to sum up and explain things so that we can better understand patterns or similarities. But you in yourself can never be summed up as an average. You are a whole and complete being and are not the sum of multiples put together and divided. To liken yourself to this, is in itself very misleading. Similarly, you are not plain or ordinary as the very fabric of your make up is unique and complexed. Your DNA, fingerprint, eye identification is completely different to anyone that has ever existed and is yet to exist on this whole entire planet. Your perception of yourself is very important, as it determines the course of your life, the route you will take and ultimately the destination in which you will arrive. Feeling mediocre can make you feel underserving and not special. However, the very essence of your being is special. Don't settle for less than your best. Demand it from yourself.

MY DAILY WOW AFFIRMATION

I am not mediocre
I am extraordinary
I am brilliant
I am wonderfully complexed
I am special

DAY 120

Positive thoughts cultivate a positive life

. . .

Stop talking yourself out of an opportunity by imagining the worst scenario taking place. You attract exactly what you put out there, you attract more opportunities by believing that despite your shortcomings you will succeed.

And if you have so much doubt and belief in your own abilities, believe in a power higher than your own, your creator lives in you. It doesn't matter how far you have gone, there is nothing that can separate you from the Love of God. Believe that the same power that God used to form you, will work through for you. That is the beauty of the greatest love of all. You have an expected end birthed from good, pure thoughts. Be reassured in this promise that your life will end out good even if it doesn't look that way now. Things can change and will change as your mind changes.

MY DAILY WOW AFFIRMATION

I will set my mind on positive things
I am getting mentally stronger
My mind is filled with peace
My mind is filled with hope
My life is improving through better thinking

DAY 121

Be the energy you want to attract

. . .

Create an environment that is conducive for your growth. Stop entertaining bad thoughts and bad energy from people that drain you, but do not add to you. You attract what you give out and what you allow. If something is not right for you, do not accept it because you feel you have allegiance to the person who gave it to you. Do not let anyone put you in a bond that you are not comfortable with. Set a standard that the people that love and respect you, are willing to adhere to. Don't compromise who you are to fit into anyone's mould. You were created to be free and to express yourself in all your fullness. To deny yourself of this is to reject who you are meant to be in this earth. Let your energy permeate the space around you and the right people will come around you.

MY DAILY WOW AFFIRMATION

I am attracting great things
My energy is fuelled by passion
I desire good for my life
Goodness is entering my life
I lack nothing good that I need

DAY 122

You inspire people who you least expect

. . .

Whether people say it or not you are inspiring them. Keep pushing to be the greatest possible version of yourself. Don't rely on the acknowledgement from others. Let your own progress motivate you and fuel you to press on despite going unrecognised. If what you are doing works, the people around you will take note. Some of them only make you aware once they have succeeded in using your methodology. How often do you thank and acknowledge those that inspire you every day? How often do you take the time to appreciate your teachers and mentors even if it is from afar? Are they fuelled by your gratitude or is it just part of their life mission to succeed? Likewise stay consistent and do not be fuelled by what people say or don't say about all the hard work you are putting in.

MY DAILY WOW AFFIRMATION

I will continue to inspire
I will aspire to encourage
I will achieve to be impactful
I will endeavour to do good deeds daily
I will pass on every lesson I learn

DAY 123

Let your smile be bright and your heart be light

. . .

Don't carry a heavy heart. Life may temporarily take an unexpected turn and it may feel like the odds are against you. However, everything in life happens for a reason. This can be to test your faith, character or strength. Challenges in life can bring to the surface things that you have not dealt with which will hinder you in your next phase of life. But do not be overcome by the difficulty that surrounds you, rather let your light radiate from within you to transform your environment. Use your God-given power to shift the temperament of your surroundings. Smile, the energy you use to smile will spread over your whole body and gradually make you feel lifted. Smile with the reassurance that things will change for the better and in your favour. Your situation will improve. Be at peace having hope that you can and will rise above any circumstance.

MY DAILY WOW AFFIRMATION

I will not let anything rob my joy
I will not let anything steal my smile
I will let my light radiate my surroundings
I will not carry a heavy heart
I will keep my spirit lifted

DAY 124

Invest in your mind, your health and your future

. . .

You are your most valuable asset. The more you invest in yourself, the more you will yield huge benefits as a result. It is important to consistently pour into yourself even when it feels like your efforts are not making any difference. Progress is not only moving forward but it is standing your ground when all odds are against you, building within you resilience, perseverance and endurance. When you have nothing left to do but to stand strong and rise, the rewards can be countless. Feeding your mind daily with positivity, affirmation and good visions of how you would like your future to be, puts you in a strong mental state which also reflects on your physical health. Doing this constantly gives you the strength and ability to do great and amazing things. There is absolutely no limit in what you can do when you keep investing in yourself.

MY DAILY WOW AFFIRMATION

I will invest in myself
I will invest in my health
I will invest in my mental state
I will value myself
I will maintain a balanced life

DAY 125

Challenges are put in your way to see if what you want is really worth the fight

. . .

It's not the end, it's just an obstacle. Don't stop until you make it. If you are on the verge of giving up, hold on to this small fact, it may not get easier, but this process will definitely make you better, stronger and wiser. Keep going, even if all this means is that you keep breathing. Don't stop fuelling yourself with the basic requirements for your survival. Breathe, eat, sleep, rest. Centre yourself in your present situation. What is the minimal thing you can do to improve the situation? This could be to do nothing and let time pass, having peace that you will not fold, crumble, bow or be destroyed. Renew your mind with affirmation to find strength from your core which you can build upon. And then fight for what you want and know is right. You will ultimately overcome if you do not give in or give up.

MY DAILY WOW AFFIRMATION

My fight is worth me overcoming
I will not crumble
I will not relent
I will stay true to myself
I am a conqueror

DAY 126

It will not always be easy, but it will always be worth it

. . .

Anything you choose to do, always count the cost. It may not be easy but whatever you put in, know that it will be worth every bit of effort you are going to make. The cost may be sleepless nights, early mornings, long days, excruciating pain, tiredness, vulnerability, isolation, being stretched, to name a few. But what you have to consider is that although it is inconvenient it is also temporary. The struggle you are going thorough is finite, it will come to an end, it will not continue forever. And while you are making payments in sweat, perhaps blood and possibly a few tears, you are gaining strength that you probably didn't even realise you had. Your pay-out will be big and last long. The struggle will be insignificant to the rewards you are about to receive, just because you were willing and took action.

MY DAILY WOW AFFIRMATION

I will continue despite the difficulty
The pain is temporary
It will all be worth it in the end
The victory will be glorious
I am anticipating a win

DAY 127

You may not know how you will do it, but know that you will get it done

. . .

Don't let the detail of how you are going to do something discourage you from doing it in the first place. The first and most important thing you need to know and be sure of is that it can be done and you are the one to do it. How you will do it, will reveal itself to you. You don't have to have the whole picture, you just need to take a few steps of faith and seek the help you need. Usually when you do not know how, it is because it is not something that you will do in isolation, there is help that you will need. Stay in pursuit of accomplishing what you have set out to do. Your pursuit will guide you to the right people and answers that you need, if what you need is not already inside of you.

MY DAILY WOW AFFIRMATION

It will all work out in the end
In the end I will be victorious
I will get to my destination
The right people will come to me
I apply my faith to my desires

DAY 128

You will be put in positions where people can see you but cannot harm you

. . .

Where you are is God ordained. No one has the power to displace you or remove you. He has placed you there for a reason and that is to accomplish your God-given purpose. Whether people like you or not and think you deserve to be there or not is none of their business or yours. Do not concern yourself with their opinions of you or feelings towards you. They may attempt to treat you in a particular way, but just know that they cannot harm you. They will only observe from afar but will not be able to manipulate or successfully devise your downfall, because they do not have the power to do so. Let their access to you be limited, they do not need to know the details of what you are doing and when you are doing it. Let them witness your rise to glory with their eyes only.

MY DAILY WOW AFFIRMATION

I am going higher
I am unstoppable
I am untouchable
Bad people are being removed from my life
I stay away from harmful people

DAY 129

Embrace what now is, let go of what was, and have faith in what will be

. . .

You can't change yesterday, but whatever you do today can affect your tomorrow. So don't stress, do whatever you need to do today to make you feel confident about your tomorrow. Be at peace with what has come and gone. Focus on what can be done right now in this moment. Do not put pressure on yourself about things that are out of your control. What will be will be, but ultimately things will work out in your favour. It is important that you believe this and prepare for it. Even in uncertainty have hope in things working out for you and be grateful for what you have now. Don't let the past or failures and mistakes weigh you down. You have learnt and grown since then, so that you can make better choices now. Trust that the choices you make will yield a good result.

MY DAILY WOW AFFIRMATION

I let go of the things I cannot control
I welcome blessings into my life
I have faith in good things happening
I believe miracles will happen in my life
I close the doors to negativity

DAY 130

You are strong not because you have no fear but because you remain unshaken in the midst of fear

. . .

Your strength is not only measured by what you have done but also by what you are doing now. Your strength is not based only on what you have overcome but also by what you are overcoming. The battle you fight today is building your strength for tomorrow, but also demonstrating the strength you have right now. You are strong and resilient when you are able to continue and push through despite the anguish you are going through right now. Keep on keeping on, I know it can be overwhelming and lonely, but if you don't give up the promise is sure, you will get there. You are powerful beyond your imagination and you won't be defeated. Continue to stand despite the opposition even if that means you are standing against your own self-doubt.

Stand strong and overcome.

MY DAILY WOW AFFIRMATION

I am strong

I am unshakeable

I am confident

I am brave

I am secure in myself

DAY 131

Don't be afraid to take risks

. . .

The biggest risk is the one you do not take. Don't be afraid to take risks and face challenges. You will never know until you know, therefore try, search, ask and take action until you know the answer you are looking for. You can recover from a fall, but a missed opportunity can lead to great regret. Even if you momentarily lose. Your loss is a lesson and every failure leads to success as long as you are willing to keep going and refuse to give up. Where you are now in life is based on daily risks that you took knowingly or unknowingly, those risks have brought you this far and you are still here. Don't make risks at someone else's expense. Take a risk to improve your situation and make things better than they are now. Don't be afraid to take another chance, but start with yourself first.

MY DAILY WOW AFFIRMATION

I am not risk adverse
I take chances
I welcome the right opportunities
I welcome lessons from losses
I am optimistic for good outcomes

DAY 132

Progress is progress

• • •

Progress is progress and consistency pays generously. Stay motivated whatever the goal may be. Small steps, big steps, as long as there is some sort of improvement and you are in a better position than you once were, this is worth celebrating. Acknowledging your progress gives you the motivation and encouragement you need to keep pressing forward. Take stock of how far you have come from where you started, even if it doesn't seem that far, it is still something. You are not where you once were and this is worth something. Better still if you can make some progress over time, you are also capable of going the full distance and seeing your journey through to the end. Stay motivated and be consistent. Whatever you did to get to where you are now, build on it and keep moving until you achieve everything you need to.

MY DAILY WOW AFFIRMATION

I am progressing daily
I am improving
I am becoming better
I am advancing
I am developing in all areas

DAY 133

Trust the timing of your life

. . .

Everything will happen in its own time. We cannot rush the hands of time neither can we slow things down. It is important to do the most you can do with the time that you have. Patience is key, stay consistent to see the change. And committed to follow the plan through. What is certain is that time will pass, what you accomplish in that time is something you can control. Be at peace that time will work in your favour, that what you need, will come to you at the right time. Whilst you wait, prepare and get ready for what you want to arrive. Don't let great opportunities pass you by with the belief that the opportunity will come again or that time will provide you with the opportunity again, trust that time has presented the opportunity now, because now is the time.

MY DAILY WOW AFFIRMATION

I trust the timing of my life
I trust my journey
I see the process to completion
I know everything will happen at the right time
I believe I will accomplish my goals

DAY 134

Go the extra mile it will be worth it

. . .

Do today what most people won't, so that you can have tomorrow what most people don't.

Most people can't be bothered, so don't be most people. Make an impact that will transform your life and possibly theirs too. Whatever you do, do it to your best ability and then some. Always give it more than you have, that way you leave yourself empty. This enables room for you to be filled with more energy, strength, light, power and a deeper essence of who you are. It enables you to be replenished because you have been stretched. Most people wouldn't do more than they have to, because they do not like inconvenience, they don't want to grow, because they do not like the weight of more responsibility. To them it appears like more work, when in actual fact it is more opportunity, more accessibility and more influence. Do more to be more.

MY DAILY WOW AFFIRMATION

I will go the extra mile
I will do more
I will go further
I will execute on all my plans
I am devoted to being my best

DAY 135

The mountain can be moved tomorrow if you lift the stones today

. . .

Everything has a start and an end. To get to the end you must start from somewhere and more often than not, that is the beginning. Do not neglect the importance of your beginning, whether it be at rock bottom or far behind everyone else. Your beginning does not have to determine where you end. It is the course of your journey that will determine where and when you eventually finish. Don't be afraid to start small and go at your own pace. You can pick up momentum when you become more familiar with what you are doing. Know that in time you will improve in your craft and will be a master of what you once were a novice at doing. The grind today is simply preparing you for the victory tomorrow.

MY DAILY WOW AFFIRMATION

I do not despise the small jobs
I am not overwhelmed by magnitude
I can do everything I commit to
I am able
I start to finish

DAY 136

Be disciplined, determined and resilient

. . .

The question is, do you love yourself enough to give yourself your best even if it means temporarily inconveniencing yourself? Do you care about your life enough to fight for it? Will you choose you, when all others abandon you? Make a choice to not give up on yourself. Be your own biggest fan and cheerleader. Encourage yourself and believe in yourself. Prove to yourself that you can and you will do it. There is a light in you, that is part of the fabric of your make up. That light is your God given-purpose. It is your gift to the world and only you can do what is needed to let it shine. It will take work, but you can do it. Get to work on yourself daily so that you can deposit seeds of discipline, determination and resilience, to reap the bountiful fruits that hard work produces later.

MY DAILY WOW AFFIRMATION

I am disciplined
I am determined
I am resilient
I have self-control
I am persistent

DAY 137

When you overcome, motivate and encourage others

. . .

We rise by helping others. If you want to go high and go far, you can't do it in isolation. You can do so much more when you have a team, rather than on your own. On your way to achieving anything in life always be gracious, offer a helping hand and be kind. You never know who is watching, and who is using you as motivation to work towards a similar goal. Be an example of how things should be done. You may not be perfect but even in your flaws there is authenticity. Something that most people can relate to. It makes you unique and it forms part of your story. As you learn from your mistakes, share your experiences so others do not have to go through the same challenges you went through.

Set the path ablaze and leave a trail for other to follow.

MY DAILY WOW AFFIRMATION

I overcome to help others do the same

I motivate

I inspire

I aspire

I teach

DAY 138

Time well spent brings much content

. . .

Make sure you spend time with the ones you love. Remember to make them feel special and let them know how valuable they are in your life. Enjoy your time in their presence, talking to them and building memories. This time is precious and not to be taken for granted, cherish it and make the most of it. Spend time working on yourself, developing your skills and preparing for the hard work to pay off. Be productive and active. Do not waste the time you have. Greatness is a collection of decisions you make over time through how you choose to spend your time and what you choose to spend your time doing. Let what you spend time on reflect where you want to be and take you there without delay.

MY DAILY WOW AFFIRMATION

I use my time effectively
I use my time as an investment in myself
I value my time
My time is precious
I am in control of my time

DAY 139

You are better than you were yesterday

. . .

Every day is an opportunity to make step by step progression towards where you want to be. Celebrate the small successes and evaluate what further steps you need to take to get closer. Take stock of where you went wrong and what you can do to improve. Invest the lessons learned from yesterday into today and the lessons of today into tomorrow. Aim to be better, by doing new things, taking on new challenges, making yourself available for growth, by being pushed beyond your current boundaries. You do not know all that you are capable of until you take the chance and explore areas beyond your comfort zone. You are more than capable of amazing things, once you dare to try to achieve them. Go for it, go get it, climb higher. It involves work, but you are able to do everything you need to do to make it happen and to succeed.

MY DAILY WOW AFFIRMATION

I am getting better daily
I am improving day by day
I am still progressing
I am reaching new heights
I am rising

DAY 140

Always believe that something wonderful awaits you

. . .

When you put your energy into hoping for something special, more often than not that particular desire gives birth to action that coincides with making those thoughts reality. What you believe ultimately shapes the life you live, it forms the person you become and sets the foundation for the choices you make as there is an expectation for a particular outcome. Having an expectation of something great happening affects your temperament, it makes you happier and motivated to do more and achieve more. It increases your capacity to endure temporary hardship because you know it will not last forever. It gives you the strength to continue and to carry on despite how dire the situation may look at the time you are going through it. Keep your hope strong, keep believing for better things to come and as you do, you create room for more.

MY DAILY WOW AFFIRMATION

I anticipate great things
Better is coming
I believe I will be victorious
I know I have achieved more than I expect
Great things are going to happen

DAY 141

Don't fear failure after taking on a risk, fear being in the same place you were because you never tried

. . .

You will not progress if you play it safe and stay in the exact same place that you have always been, by doing the exact thing you have always done. Being in the same place at times can be like going backwards, because other people have moved forward and progressed and moved ahead. The world is in constant motion, staying still over long periods of time is regression. The fear of falling or failing is not to be compared to staying in the same place because even in failing you learn. There is progression in learning, because you have gained knowledge that you did not once have, therefore you are already ahead. You can then use this knowledge to propel you forward. If you fail several times, you learn several lessons. The more you learn the less you fail, the more you progress.

MY DAILY WOW AFFIRMATION

I will always keep trying
I will keep progressing
I will stay focused
I am not easily distracted
I am moving forward

DAY 142

Through your persistence you gain it, through your consistency you own it

. . .

How many doors do you think you have to knock on, for the door you want to finally be open to you? How many attempts do you have to make before you get the answer you need to resolve the problem you are facing? How long do you have to search for what you are looking for before you find exactly what it is that you want? How many years does it take to master a specialist craft? The truth is there is not a set number, if you want to achieve great success you will knock on as many doors as you need to knock on, until the door is open to you. You will keep trying until your efforts yield a result. You will keep searching until you find the answer. You cannot be consumed by how long it takes, but rather be willing to do whatever it takes.

MY DAILY WOW AFFIRMATION

I am persistent

I am consistent

I am pursuant

I will not stop until I win

I will stay on track

DAY 143

What is yours is yours

. . .

Do not let anyone discourage you from claiming what rightfully belongs to you. It is within your interest to do whatever it takes to redeem it. You may even need to fight for it, so do not be afraid. There are people that will challenge your ownership of peace. Don't let them steal this from you. Fight for it, it is yours and you are deserving of keeping it. Your peace is important, your confidence is important, your self-worth is important, and you have the right to have all these things and more. It belongs to you, it is yours and what is for you, no one has the right to take from you. Be bold and stand secure in claiming these things and more. Someone else's peace shouldn't rob you of yours. Go for everything that belongs to you. Stand your ground and own it.

MY DAILY WOW AFFIRMATION

What is mine will not pass me by
I will receive every blessing that belongs to be
I will achieve my goals
I will not miss out on what is mine
I will reclaim every good thing that is mine

DAY 144

Don't give up on your goal because of a setback

. . .

Giving up on your goals because of a temporary setback is like slashing the other three tyres of your vehicle because you get one flat. Do not destroy everything because something has gone wrong. Instead make the effort to fix the problem. Living in a generation that throws things away rather than fix things, can lead to wasted effort, wasted energy and wasted resource. Use what you already have to get you ahead. Giving up can make matters worse or set you behind. Each time you fail or fall get back up, don't stay there. Keep going no matter how slow it takes. Get help along the way to finish the journey. But whatever you do, don't stop, don't give up, don't give in. Bad things happen to everybody, look up and get up.

MY DAILY WOW AFFIRMATION

I will not give up
I will not let setbacks hold me back
I will move forward
I will attain great success
I will achieve my goals

DAY 145

Without the fight there is no victory

. . .

There is no glory without some sort of challenge or struggle, there is no success without overcoming or solving some sort of problem. Don't fear the struggle anticipate the victory. Keep your mind fixed on the glory, the success, the accomplishment, the achievement. How it feels, what it will mean to you, how it will impact and touch the lives of those around you and beyond. Having a focus on a positive outcome, gives you the strength you need to get through the challenge and the battle. Predicting how it all ends in your favour, gives you a sense of joy and additional energy to get through what could appear like serious difficulty. Your victory is the light at the end of the tunnel, keep believing that it is in front of you and every effort you make brings you one step closer to getting there.

MY DAILY WOW AFFIRMATION

The battle will be worth it
The victory will be glorious
I will fight to win
I am a conqueror
I will be victorious

DAY 146

Don't rush the process, everything will happen at the right on time

. . .

Don't rush the hands of time as what you want needs to go through the necessary process before it reaches you. There may also be a process that you need to go through so that you are ready for this new responsibility. Do not rush, at times what is meant to help you can end up hurting you if it comes into your life at the wrong time. Or you can end up destroying things if you are not equipped with the necessary tools you need, before it is in your possession. So, wait patiently. What is for you will come at the right time. You will be ready and equipped to give it the value it is worth. Do not get discouraged or complacent. What is for you is on the way, wait for it, stay with it, stick to it. Don't give up on it.

MY DAILY WOW AFFIRMATION

I will wait patiently for my blessings
I will not rush my process
I am becoming better daily
I submit to my journey
I am becoming more disciplined

DAY 147

Be thankful for what you are now, and keep fighting for what you want to become

. . .

You are all you are because the work you have put in over time. Celebrate who you are, your intelligence, your work ethic, your determination, your persistence and resilience, your attitude to becoming and improving. These are wonderful characteristics. Think about all the effort you've made to achieve the very many things you have accomplished. There are people who are in less favourable positions because they were not willing or were unable to do what it takes to make progress. Yes, indeed you are not where you want to be, but you are not where you were. But because you have made it this far, you are deserving of making it all the way. Do not stop now, do whatever it takes to feel that sense of freedom with the knowledge you have gone the full course and no longer need to work for what you have.

MY DAILY WOW AFFIRMATION

I am grateful for all I have
I am thankful for where I am now
I am excited about where I am going
I am fighting to be all that I can be
I will achieve greatness

DAY 148

There may be obstacles, mistakes, setbacks, but with hard work you will be limitless

. . .

You are stronger than you think, you can overcome anything if you keep going and don't give up. Anything worth having has a cost attached to it, this just makes it more valuable because it does not come easy, not everyone has access to it, or can obtain it. Achieving anything in life that does not come easy, will involve challenges, there will be lessons to be learnt and temporary setbacks, however if you stay the length of the course, there you will be victorious and the victory cannot be compared to the brief struggle. And in addition to being successful, you add value to yourself, there is no limit to how much you increase in value as you have developed, your growth is exponential and has no bounds. So, despite the struggle remember the great things that lie ahead of you.

MY DAILY WOW AFFIRMATION

I will overcome the obstacles
I will learn from my mistakes
I have limitless potential
I am on the way to greatness
I am operating at my best

DAY 149

Use your story as a key to unlock someone's prison

. . .

Your story is something captured in time to inform, to encourage and to learn from. There may be parts to your story that you are ashamed of or that you wish did not happen, parts in which you wish you could do over. But take heart, every part of your story happened for a reason and there is someone out there that has gone through the same thing or perhaps even worse. Furthermore, there is someone going through the challenges you have overcome, and they need to know it is possible to make it out on the other side. They need to know that there is really a light at the end of the tunnel, that the miracle they need is possible. You are proof of that miracle, you are the key to unlock that door, the light at the end of the tunnel. Your story is their hope.

MY DAILY WOW AFFIRMATION

I will share my lessons
I will share my blessings
I am the answer to someone's prayer
I am a solution to someone's problem
I am a problem solver

DAY 150

Live a life you chose, not a life you settled for

. . .

Every day you make decisions. You choose your preference, or you choose to do nothing and leave your life in the hands of those around you. When you leave your life to fate, it may not always work in your favour. There may be things that you have to settle with because you didn't make known what you wanted, so you were given whatever was available. Whatever is available may not be what is best for you. Be clear on what you want out of life and fight for it. Choose what works for you and serves your best interest. Live a purposeful intentional life where you do not settle, but you create based on what you require and need to fulfil your desires. Choose happiness, choose peace, choose freedom all of which are not passive you have to actively pursue these things to obtain them in life.

MY DAILY WOW AFFIRMATION

I do not settle for less
I chose to live a full life
I will always strive for more
I am grateful
I am thankful

DAY 151

Excuses are useless, results are invaluable

. . .

Momentary discomfort can never be compared to a lifetime of reward. Doing something that can change the whole trajectory of your life will always be worth it. Do not talk yourself out of something more amazing than you can ever imagine just because it takes you out of your comfort zone. Do not delay achieving greatness because you will have to go through brief difficulty. Do not give yourself excuses to remain in the same place. Be willing to be stretched, to grow, to become more than what you are now. You are capable of wonderful things, without restriction or limitation. Work to become those amazing things, to add limitless value to yourself. Whatever the price you have to pay, you will be paid back in full, countless times over. In comparison the price you paid will be insignificant and will not even be remembered.

MY DAILY WOW AFFIRMATION

I will be result orientated
I will be solutions orientated
I will be optimistic
I will apply my intelligence to every situation
I will use my skill

DAY 152

Stop explaining yourself to people and just do what works for you

. . .

No matter how hard you try, you will never be able to please everyone. It will always leave you feeling depleted and empty. Nothing is deserving of making you feel worthless, so don't. The only person worth pleasing is yourself. One of the most important people you have to answer to is yourself. When all is said and done, what you think of yourself is very important. Don't compromise who you are for anyone. Stand secure in who you are and whose you are. You are royalty, stronger and wiser than you know. What people think or say about you does not automatically turn you into these things. Their opinion of you doesn't change who you are, and it shouldn't change the way you feel about yourself. Identify who you want to be in the world and walk as such, your power and capabilities are limitless.

MY DAILY WOW AFFIRMATION

I do not need the validation of anyone
I do not need to give an explanation for my greatness
I validate myself
I embrace my gift
I honour the power of fulfilling purpose

DAY 153

Keep fighting for what you believe is right even if most people don't understand

. . .

The battle you are fighting may not be everyone's battle. They are not obligated to fight for and with you and that is ok. Likewise, only because they do not understand the battle you are facing it doesn't mean it is not a worthy cause. Do not let anyone discourage you from doing what you know is right. The energy that you are pouring into it is valid. Keep fighting the good fight, in the end when you win the purpose may be revealed to them and even if it isn't, you know why you are fighting and that is the most important thing. Your struggle may not be their struggle, your fight may not be their fight, your obstacle may not be their obstacle, but this doesn't mean it makes it any less meaningful. Keep your head high, push through, do all you can to overcome, because the cost of winning rests on your shoulders.

MY DAILY WOW AFFIRMATION

I stand for what is right
I am not afraid to stand alone if I have to
My ideology is valid
My thoughts are precious
I am deserving of respect

DAY 154

The present you are constructing should look like the future you are dreaming

. . .

It is important to make sure that you are laying the right foundations today for your tomorrow. Do your current choices align with your goals, visions and aspirations? Every step you take is either bringing you closer to where you want to be or taking you further away, so act wisely. Always have your goals in mind. Always reflect on where you want to be and whether where you are now serves the purpose for which you are working towards. This requires you to be honest with yourself. It requires you to be disciplined. Sometimes you may not feel like going that extra mile or following through with certain disciplines because it doesn't gratify your self-indulgence. But to combat this, factor in rest and leisure into your journey, this is if it does not distract or take you off course. But do not prioritise rest and leisure over the work that you know you need to do.

MY DAILY WOW AFFIRMATION

I am working on a great future
My future looks bright
I believe my future will be amazing
I am working hard now to enjoy later
I am creating balance

DAY 155

You cannot have what you refuse to build

. . .

If you want it, lay the right foundations and build on it. Don't expect for things that you have not worked for. If you are not willing to do what it takes to get the results you want or require, don't demand or expect it to happen. You cannot expect to get results, if you do not put the work in. Whatever you want in life, be willing to put the work in. Be willing to make the sacrifice, be willing to put in the time. Don't look at other's success and achievement and want the same for yourself without doing what they did to get what they are now enjoying. You should have the expectation that you may have to do even more to get the same results, because you do not have their knowledge or experience. Give more expect less, and therefore keep giving, keep doing, keep working.

MY DAILY WOW AFFIRMATION

I am building the future I want to see
I believe in my future
I will succeed
I will not go off track
I am building something that will last

DAY 156

Each day is a chance for you to start over

. . .

If you have to face failure every day until you finally succeed, it's worth it. Do not think that you have to continue with something when it is clear that it is not working for you. Every day offers a new opportunity to start fresh. So, forget the mistakes of the past and use them as a lesson and stepping stone to prepare you for what is ahead. You do not need to feel stuck, you can try again. It is not over, until it is over. And it is rarely over until you win. You are still on this journey, therefore there is still a chance to make it. You may not win the first time round, maybe not the second, third or the hundredth time but a time will come when it will be your turn, this time is more likely to come sooner if you do not give up.

MY DAILY WOW AFFIRMATION

I start with hope that I will succeed
I am building a solid foundation
I am starting with confidence that I will finish strong
I am grateful for each day
I am grateful for each opportunity to start again

DAY 157

The opportunity to rebuild is in the breaking

. . .

Breaking is not always a bad thing. Stopping and starting again is at times the best thing you can ever do. Check where you are. Is this really working for you? Is this ultimately serving your purpose? Is this going to bring you closer to achieving your goals and aspirations in life? Are you growing? Are you becoming better? Stronger? Wiser? Will starting over give you the opportunity to build a better foundation so that what you are doing will last? Be honest with yourself. Don't give into the shame associated with starting again or being broken. Remember it is only for a short while, you will come back stronger and be able to go further. Trust in your ability to transform, to grow and develop from the adversity. You will rise again. You can and will get pass this and become better than before.

MY DAILY WOW AFFIRMATION

I am rebuilding to be stronger than ever
The struggle is temporary
I am transforming into the person I want to be
I am working on my self-improvement
I am rebuilding something unshakeable

DAY 158

You are the author of your own story

. . .

Write the story of your life. Don't let anyone dictate how your story ends and which direction it should go in. You are the author, you have the pen. Every day is a blank page that needs to be filled. What decisions will you make to enable this story to be a true depiction of the person you want the world to know and see? Write it down. Who do you want to touch? What lives do you want to impact? What do you want people to understand that they never knew before? You have the power to inform, to teach and to show the world something completely new that they had no insight into before, because no one can ever tell your story like you. It is completely unique to you even if there are similarities and common themes shared elsewhere, your life is your story to the world.

MY DAILY WOW AFFIRMATION

I am the author of my own destiny
I am the creator of my vision
I am the director of my journey
I have the power to make decisions that serve me
I control which way I choose to take

DAY 159

May God comfort you with love and refill your heart with peace

. . .

There may be some very dark and lonely times in your life that you will have to go through. Where fear and anxiety seek to overcome you. I pray that every ounce of fear, anxiety, and discouragement will be taken away and that an unexplainable peace will overwhelm you. I pray calm to every raging storm and quiet to the sounds of thunder that fill you with despair. This is not your end, you will make it, in fact you must. There is so much more for you on the other side of this place that you are in. And although, what you are going through is very real, very painful and very scary, it will pass. You will see better days, there is light and there is joy to be experienced. You may feel empty, but you have hope, grab it and lean into it, let it surround and fill you.

Better is coming.

MY DAILY WOW AFFIRMATION

I am comforted by God's peace
My heart is at rest
I have hope
I do not give in to anxiety
I have faith everything will work out

DAY 160

Faith makes things possible it does not make things disappear

. . .

Your faith is the catalyst to make things that are yet to exist a reality. Work is involved, there is no escaping that, you can't get something for nothing, you must give of yourself a payment for what you wish to receive. However, if you are willing to pay the price, to make the sacrifice and to put in the work, you are deserving of the great and wonderful things that will happen because you had faith enough to believe it. Faith doesn't dispel the work you have to do, it gives you the strength to do it. Faith does not discount the sleepless nights, it gives you the energy to stay awake. Believing in the impossible, doesn't make it any less difficult to achieve, it simply makes what once was unattainable, attainable and possible. Because you chose to see a problem that could be overcome, you can find the solution.

MY DAILY WOW AFFIRMATION

I have faith in my future
I believe my dreams are possible
I pursue my goals with faith
I trust I will attain everything I work for
I am working hard for what I want to achieve

DAY 161

Commit yourself to excellence

. . .

Excellence is not inherited; it is something you work hard towards. To achieve the highest standard demands the greatest level of effort. Excellence speaks of itself; it demonstrates discipline, detail, high quality and skill. Anything you do, do it in a way that it produces something of optimum value. What is the relevance of the effort you put into making something, if it does not add up to much and no one can see its value? Aim to be and produce your best. Demand of yourself your best, be committed to delivering excellence in all you do and give. Do not compromise your standards, don't settle, don't give the minimum, give the maximum. Go for the best and be the best. Rise higher than your previous attempt, continue to produce better and more. Be competitive not with those around you but against yourself. Do better and more than you did before.

MY DAILY WOW AFFIRMATION

I commit to excellence
I am striving to give my best
I will do my best
I am sharpening my skills
I am excelling in my ability

DAY 162

Walk away from things that do not serve your purpose

• • •

Your purpose is what you were created for, it is the reason for you being on this earth, the gift you are sharing with the world. If you know what your purpose is, and there is something stopping you from achieving it, remove the hindrance or find another way to fulfil your purpose. But do not let anything block or stop you from living a purposeful life. Don't be robbed of your value. Your sense of value is important, it is part of what keeps you centred and motivated to continue, don't allow a person or a situation to rob you of this. You are stronger when you walk away and remove yourself from things that have ill-will towards you. Don't reside in harm's way, be active in protecting what really matters and your purpose and peace are part of this.

MY DAILY WOW AFFIRMATION

I am walking towards my destination
I am walking away from distractions
I am focused
I am taking each step at a time
I am actively pursuant of purpose

DAY 163

There is a solution to every problem

. . .

Be encouraged there is a solution, you don't have to suffer, struggle or fight in vain. Keep going until you get it. Don't give up, don't relent. You have not come this far to end up with nothing. Get your answer, get what you are searching for, the very thing that you came all this way to receive, make sure you get it. Get the help you need to get to it, if necessary. Ask the right questions to the right people. Keep digging, keep exploring, someone is depending on you to bring the answer to light, to uncover and expose it. The answer is there, what you are searching for exists, you just have to keep looking. Keep hoping, believing and trusting. You are not going insane or mad, you just have the insight that has not been uncovered by anyone else yet. The answer is around you, it is not far from you.

MY DAILY WOW AFFIRMATION

I am confident that every problem has a solution
I am optimistic about the outcome
I am getting the job done
I am doing what I need to do
I will not give up

DAY 164

You have been assigned this battle to show others it can be won

. . .

Don't get frustrated for having to always be strong, always having to fight, always having to face a challenge.

Life has assigned you the opportunity to rise and be great. When you win and claim the victory the pain of yesterday will be forgotten. But you will be remembered, your victory is your legacy. There are people waiting and depending on your success. Hold on, stand strong, stay with it. Do not lose hope. This battle can be won, this mountain can be moved, this challenge can be overcome. And you can and will be the one to do it. Everything you have been through up until this point has prepared you for what it is that you are facing. Remember how you overcame that fear you once had. Remember when you started, how many mistakes you made and now you can do it without even thinking about it.
Apply those principles now, it will serve you well.

MY DAILY WOW AFFIRMATION

I have everything it takes to win the battle
I will not be fazed by the obstacle
I will be victorious
I will overcome
I will win

191

DAY 165

Remember that great things take time

. . .

You are a work in progress. It didn't take one day to bring you to where you are now, so to get to where you want to be, will not happen overnight. Take the time to reflect on your goals, what you achieved and what you are still working on. Don't be discouraged about not ticking every box. Be encouraged that there is still hope, once you have air in your lungs you can do whatever it takes to make whatever you need to do happen. You are able and what you want is possible. Everything worth having is worth the wait it takes to receive it. So appreciate the time it is taking, appreciate the progress, enjoy the small improvements and even celebrate them. Value the growth that is taking place within you while you wait, the person you are becoming is commendable, strong and wonderful. What you are doing is worthwhile and significant so enjoy the process.

MY DAILY WOW AFFIRMATION

I am willing to wait for the greatness that awaits me
I will not be discouraged by delay
I know that with time things will work out
I am growing in all areas
I will achieve

DAY 166

Success comes from what you do consistently not what you do occasionally

. . .

Success comes from being persistent and consistent no matter what you face. You are not successful until you accomplish what you set out to do in an appropriate time from when you started. By constantly stopping and starting, you will not achieve anything within an appropriate time, you need to pace yourself, which may require that you go slower at times and then speed the process up at other times by applying more effort, but what is key is that you continue and maintain momentum. If you want to win you have to give your best and keep giving your best until you obtain the results that you desire. To only give your best when you feel like it, will not produce results of the highest value because you withheld effort that could have contributed to you going further, faster or being more effective. Maintain composure and strive for excellence

MY DAILY WOW AFFIRMATION

I am consistent
I am building good habits
I am adopting good character
I am active with my goals
I am intentional with my desires

DAY 167

It is in your weakest moment that you are your strongest

. . .

When you feel weak, you give more than what you believe you have. It is at this point you are actually at your strongest and you are only getting stronger by pushing yourself and stretching yourself. You are expanding your capacity for more, to do more and to be more. Do not bow down, do not give in, pull from your reserve; the part of you that is stored deep down inside of you, where the energy you need to get over that last hurdle is. You can do it, but you have to believe that you can. Do not give in to the tiredness, the voice that says you can't or that it is impossible. Your body will follow where your mind takes it, if it is compelling enough. Give it all you have until you literally have nothing left to give. Show your real strength not your weakness.

MY DAILY WOW AFFIRMATION

When I feel weak, I am strong
I will not stop
I will push through
I am being stretched to expand my reach
I am overcoming every challenge

DAY 168

The secret of your future success is uncovered in your daily routine

. . .

What you think, is revealed in what you say, your words over time influence the decisions you make and actions you take. Repetitive actions over time becomes habit, your habits structure the foundation of your character and your character ultimately forms the basis of who you are as a person. What do your thoughts currently say about the person you are going to become and the types of things you are going to do? If this is not reflective of what you want them to be. You can change them right now. Cultivate thoughts that will create the future you actually want to live in. Then start speaking it into existence trusting that your words will follow with action. Once you've made the first few steps create momentum through consistency and with time what started as a thought will be the reality you live.

MY DAILY WOW AFFIRMATION

I commit to daily progression
I am improving my daily habits
I am building stronger character
I am mastering my day
I am cultivating a good attitude

DAY 169

Face your fears

. . .

What you fear will not disappear until you confront it. That monster under the bed will either stay there forever or will turn out to be a sock that escaped the wash. But you will never know until you face it head on. Being fearful is not going to make it go away. But addressing it will resolve the situation. You may have a very valid reason to fear as your life or the life of someone that you care about may be in danger. Nonetheless being afraid will not save your life or theirs, however action will. It is important to think about what you can do to combat your fear. It can be as simple as switching on the light, so that you can see clearly and expose things for what they really are, therefore getting the answers you need. Whatever it is, do it and do not delay.

MY DAILY WOW AFFIRMATION

I am facing my fears
I am not limited by my fears
I will not run away from conflict
I can cope with negative situations
I can manage my expectations

DAY 170

Don't expect to see a change if you don't make one

. . .

Things change as a result of activity, it requires action. What are you willing to do to see the change you desire? Even the smallest change can make a significant difference to the course of your life. But you have to be prepared to take action and take that action consistently. It is not good enough to start today and stop tomorrow, because that may undo the work that you have done. When you start making these changes, you can expect to see steady differences occur in your life over time, these may even happen immediately or may take a while. The change will certainly happen when you put the necessary effort in. If it takes some time for you to see anything, this is not the time to stop or be discouraged, continue to be consistent with your efforts. It will pay off in the end and the pay-out will be substantial.

MY DAILY WOW AFFIRMATION

I am making positive changes
I am making consistent progressive action
I will continue to make steady improvement
I am preparing for better
I know that hard work pays off

DAY 171

You will get through this

. . .

Even if it seems overwhelming and impossible, be confident in the fact that you will pull through and make it to the other side. Don't put too much pressure on yourself. It looks hard now, but persevere you will get through this. Difficulty can often be misleading as it will appear that overcoming the challenge is unachievable. However more often than not, you do combat and win. In fact, sometimes when you are even in the midst of the challenge and you are overcoming, you may feel like you will not see it through to the end, even though you are actively pressing forward. Don't entertain discouragement or feelings of defeat, they are deceivers, designed to take you off track, you can and you will most certainly get through this and be testament that it can be done.

MY DAILY WOW AFFIRMATION

I will get through this
I am a conqueror
I am victorious
I am stronger than this
I will not give up

DAY 172

Become conscious of what is really worth your time and energy

. . .

Keep your focus strong. If whatever you are doing is not for your rise, it is merely wasting your energy and needs to be stopped. You cannot afford to waste your time and energy on things that do not benefit the person you want to be in life. To get there in the first place, demands so much effort invested over time, so wasting it will only hold you back. You are wise and intelligent enough to know what is not working for you. Do not go through the motions or worry about upsetting people. If they are for you, they will understand why you have to make decisions that favour where you are going. Be wary of people that will prefer you to stay exactly where you are. Don't allow them to restrict you by taking up your time. Focus your energy on where you are going and things that will propel you forward.

MY DAILY WOW AFFIRMATION

I am becoming more self-ware
I am learning what is best for me
I will protect my energy
My time is valuable
I will reserve my energy

DAY 173

Feed your faith starve your doubt

. . .

If it nourishes you and fills you with hope, continue to allow these things to feed your mind and spirit.

If it depletes your energy and robs you of your self-belief and joy, remove it from your life immediately. The environments that you are in, what you watch, read and listen to all feed you consciously or subconsciously. You have to be careful to make sure you are taking in the right things that will aid you in becoming all that you hope to be. The company you keep naturally will pour into you and influence the decisions you make. You have to surround yourself with people that are going in the same direction as you and are happy for your growth and rise. Having the right energy around you motivates you to continue and gives you the strength to go on. Make sure the energy around you is right.

MY DAILY WOW AFFIRMATION

I act in faith
I do not allow doubt to stop me
I have self-belief
I surround myself with positivity
I have a can-do attitude

DAY 174

Failure is another stepping stone to greatness

. . .

Fail, fail and fail again. Every failure is a step closer to the answer you need. Learn from it and do not be afraid of it. Failure is inevitable. Be ok to fail. It is not a bad thing and its negative effects are momentary, however its benefits are long-lived. Your failure does not define you, what you do after you fail does. The biggest failures are the most successful, because they had to fail until they could fail no more, until they received all the knowledge they could from the mistakes they made. Failure serves its purpose in your life. It is important to know how to fail, to know how to get it wrong so that you know how to get it right. It also keeps you humble and prevents you from getting complacent. If you do not make mistakes you will not value the cost of making the right decision.

MY DAILY WOW AFFIRMATION

I use my past failures as stepping stones
I learn from my mistakes
I am becoming wiser
I am becoming better
I am becoming stronger

DAY 175

Failure is not final or permanent

. . .

Get up and try again. keep trying until you get it right. When you get it right, show others the way, so they do not make the same mistakes that you made. Blaze trails, create pathways and pass out keys to locked doors no one else has access to but you. You rise by lifting others and you stand on the shoulders of the people that went before you. The difficulty they faced was so that you could have a more straightforward journey. You would not be where you are if it was not for their sacrifice, so pay it forward and give to those coming behind you. Don't worry about how it looks if you don't get everything right, perfection is an illusion. The reason you made it this far is because someone gave you hope and with that hope you won. Give hope, help others win.

MY DAILY WOW AFFIRMATION

Failure is temporary
I am not defeated
I will win
I will continue until I win
I will strive to be victorious

DAY 176

Even if the weapons form, they will never prosper

. . .

Whatever is designed for your downfall will not prosper. However, the same people that are plotting your demise will witness your elevation and rise. They cannot stand your success and progress and that is not your business, so focus on what is and that is, keep moving forward. Let their hatred for you eat away at them and let them eventually destroy themselves. Feel no ill-will towards them as this does not add to you in anyway. Continue to be good and to do good, be kind to everyone, but know who and who is not deserving of your time and energy. Justice will always prevail over injustice even if for a while it doesn't appear that way. The truth will always be revealed and overthrow deceit. Darkness can never overcome light, so always let your light shine, don't let it be dimmed and do not let your voice be silenced.

MY DAILY WOW AFFIRMATION

Anything against my progression will not overcome me
I will not be stopped by negative people
I will continue to rise
I will continue to succeed
I am out of the reach of those that mean me harm

DAY 177

What is coming is better than what has gone

. . .

You are not missing out if something has come and gone. The absence of something in your life creates room for more. It leaves a void that requires the right thing to fill it. Be expectant of great things to come. You need to let go of the old to give way to the new. Do a mental, emotional and physical clear out. Get rid of the junk in your life that is taking up space. Remove things that are weighing you down that have been there for years. Move on, you have outgrown these things. It's time to welcome better into your life. You may need to change environment and move into a new place to accommodate better things. Take that leap of faith and move, go to where you will grow and bear fruit, where you will see the evidence of your hard work.

MY DAILY WOW AFFIRMATION

Better is coming in my life
Abundance is on the way to find me
Blessings are heading my way
I have emotional balance
I have complete peace

DAY 178

Your elevation may require your isolation

. . .

Do whatever is necessary to get to that next level, sometimes that means doing it by yourself, saying no to things that distract you or steer you in a different direction. It may involve blocking out the doubt to protect your energy at all cost, by staying away. Everyone is not going to understand where it is that you are going and why you are going there. They may not understand how important it is and why you are spending so much of your time and energy focusing on achieving and accomplishing what it is that you are trying to do. Although it is a lonely place to be and it is hard at times to feel motivated, it is a necessary process. You cannot be dependent on anyone or anything to take you to where you are going, you must be self-sufficient. Always remember you are enough.

MY DAILY WOW AFFIRMATION

I am not afraid to stand alone
I am self-sufficient
I am being elevated
I am rising
I am going higher

DAY 179

Your best is on its way

. . .

Don't think that what has gone was your best and that you cannot do any better. Don't obsess over your past in hope to relive what once was. Everything happens in stages, and at that time, what you experienced and went through was important for you at that time. But what you need in the future is what is best for you right now and if you do what is required of you, commit to excellence and remain consistent, the best of what you need will come. Be expectant for your efforts to produce the results you desire, this will put you in a place fit for where you need to be. You have the necessary tools inside of you, study, understand and use them for your advantage. You are becoming better so naturally you will obtain better results. Trust your ability to become even more great than you are now.

MY DAILY WOW AFFIRMATION

The best is awaiting me
I will continue to strive for the best
Better days are coming
The sun will shine on all my endeavours
I will commit to excellence

DAY 180

Trust and wait for what is still unseen

. . .

Only because you cannot yet see it, doesn't mean it is not real or is does not exist. It does not mean it is incapable of happening because you have not seen it with your eyes or touched it with your hands. Your dream has every ability to be tangible. Many of the things that you are enjoying today are the dreams of people that decided to trust that their dreams could be a reality and could serve the lives of many. Therefore, trust the power of your dream serving many. Something that can be a fleeting thought can one day change the world and how things are done. Do not disregard the impact your dream can have when you trust its development into something physical for all to see. It will take time and work, but everything will work, everything always does.

MY DAILY WOW AFFIRMATION

I trust the path I am walking on
I will reach my destination
I will not miss my way
I am divinely directed
I walk in faith

DAY 181

Your light will cause people and opportunities to pursue you

. . .

Focus on fulfilling purpose. The opportunities will come, the help will come, the doors will open. Stay focused and be your authentic self. Who you are radiates from within you. Find your passion and let it set your heart ablaze. It doesn't need to make noise or have a big bang, its beauty is in you activating it. Activate your light, your gift to the world. Once you do, whoever needs to find you will find you. Whatever help you need will be made available to you. Work on yourself and your craft diligently, the right opportunities will come. Your light will direct the right people to you. Even if for a while you feel like you are being overlooked and underrated, your time will come. Remain consistent, show your commitment and your work will speak for itself.

MY DAILY WOW AFFIRMATION

I am a light
My gift will shine
I will attract favour
I am blessed
The right people will contact me

DAY 182

Sometimes good things fall apart so better things can fall together

. . .

Let go of the good for the great. Don't settle for mediocrity. Be more than you are so you can make a greater impact. It may feel hurtful at first when something good does not work out, but trust that what is yours will find you. And what is yours is best for you. Better things are coming. Things are falling in place in your favour to help you achieve your goals. You are growing and getting stronger every day. Your faith is being built up so that you can believe in bigger dreams and see them come to pass. At times when it feels like things don't work out, it is actually in your favour, because what you may have desired could have been harmful to you or delayed your progression. Just know that what you need is making itself available to you so remain encouraged and motivated.

MY DAILY WOW AFFIRMATION

I will not miss my blessings
I will not settle for good when I can have the best
I will achieve to the best standards
I am expectant of miracles
I am hopeful for the best

DAY 183

You were given the dream because you have what it takes to make it happen

. . .

Your purpose can be a mandate or a calling. Something that you are passionate about and think about constantly. It's not a coincidence or by chance. What you hope for and dream is in you because you are supposed to make it happen. And furthermore, you have the tools to do just that. You may require help along the way, but ultimately you are the one needed to make your dream a reality. If you are wondering where to start, start with yourself, renew your thought process. Believe and convince yourself that it can happen, because it absolutely can. Your dream is so important in unlocking the dreams of others if you are brave enough to pursue it. It doesn't come easy and it is a very scary task to undertake, but it is possible and can definitely be done once you believe in yourself.

MY DAILY WOW AFFIRMATION

My dream is significant
I will not take my calling lightly
I will do whatever I can to realise my dream
I believe in my vision
I believe my dreams will happen

DAY 184

It will all be worth it in the end

. . .

It is in the darkest storm that the light of hope shines brightest. When you are going through your lowest, darkest moments remember the light of hope. Allow it to guide you and give you comfort. Allow it to reassure you and give you peace. Everything will work out. It will all be ok in the end. Everything you are going through is for a worthy cause. Who you are becoming is great. Where you are going is great and you are setting a legacy that will outlive you. People will hear of your story and believe that they too can make it. People will believe because you chose not to give up. Your faith is so critical for the rest of the journey. People that you do not know will find inspiration from your determination and will not give up in the midst of hardship. Do not lose hope and do not give up.

MY DAILY WOW AFFIRMATION

My vision is worth the fight
My goals are worth my pursuit
I value the gift inside of me
I am grateful I was chosen to use this gift
I will see my journey through to the end

DAY 185

Live with a relentless pursuit of better

. . .

Don't settle, you have not worked so hard, sacrificed so much and exercised so much discipline, for you not to reap the full rewards of your effort. Just like you have been adamant in your pursuit to achieve, be adamant about wanting the best and not accepting anything less. You have been giving your best, why shouldn't you expect the best back. As you work hard on yourself to improve, you are developing every day. With that level of growth, you can expect to see even more growth in what you do and who you are becoming. Desire to be better than you were yesterday. As your value increases, you can demand more for the things you do and invest in better tools to assist you. In doing this you add to your confidence in your ability to achieve.

MY DAILY WOW AFFIRMATION

I am relentless
I am pursuant
I am working towards better
I am committed to growth
I am determined to achieve

DAY 186

Don't doubt yourself, do what it takes to make it happen

. . .

Anything is possible to the believer. Be unwavering and even if you have an ounce of doubt, don't let it stop you. Let your faith keep you moving forward in hope that it may just happen for you one day. If anyone can do it, you can. Stop doubting yourself and talking yourself out of many opportunities for fear of failure. You won't know unless you try and realise that it is possible. You may have to try a few times before you get the results that you want, but at least you are closer to achieving your goals and more confident in your ability to succeed than before. Stop allowing your fears to limit and restrict you, there is so much more that you can do on the other side of fear. Take a chance on yourself, all the investment that you have made has to count for something.

MY DAILY WOW AFFIRMATION

I believe in myself
I will do what it takes to make it happen
I will not fail
I will not be restricted by fear
I am closer to achieving my goals

DAY 187

Prayer works

. . .

Whether you are religious or not, believe in God or not. Your prayers do not fall to the ground and go unanswered. Prayer has the power to change things, to make things that never existed start to form. It is you taking what is not and making it into something through faith. It allows you to centralise your thoughts and focus your energy. It is a surrender from yourself to a force bigger than you. This way you are no longer responsible for the burden of what it is that you are requesting. It is out of your hands and by faith you believe the result will work out in your favour. When you have done all else and you literally can do no more; pray. Prayer gives you peace, it reassures you that your efforts are not in vain and that all hope is not loss.

MY DAILY WOW AFFIRMATION

My prayers are being answered
I am applying my faith to actions
I trust that I will get what I work for
I believe I will achieve
I believe in the power I possess

DAY 188

When God is for you, don't bother yourself about who is against you, you are on the winning side

. . .

The same God that gave you life and that is lovingly watching over you and rooting for your success, is also standing in your corner desiring the best for you. God wants you to be happy, to have peace, to have love. God wants for you to make it and is not waiting for your demise. So know that you have heaven backing you in your endeavours, to make life better for others while you work hard on yourself. Those that want to see you fall and fail will only see you rise and succeed. No matter how many times they try to slam the door in your face, another door will open. When they try to destroy your opportunities, better and bigger opportunities will come to you. Don't let the people that are trying to bring you down discourage you. There is a more powerful force fighting for you.

MY DAILY WOW AFFIRMATION

I am divinely protected
I do not live in fear
I am confident that I will be successful
I am loved
I am cherished

DAY 189

Life is tough but not as tough as you

. . .

You are stronger than you know. Show life that pressure makes you unbreakable. You will not bow, you will not give in, you will not fall to the ground and beg. Instead you will stand tall, you will rise, you will grow stronger. Life can be challenging, that if you are not rooted in faith, you can have the life knocked out of you. But it is important not to be reactive to external changes as they will constantly lead you down a slippery slope of despair and powerlessness. Rather stand firm on what you know and take hold of your faith, what you understand to be true. You can and will get through every trial, you have everything within you that you need to succeed. You are worthy of the greatness that is about to happen in your life. You will make it and you will win.

MY DAILY WOW AFFIRMATION

I am stronger than my challenge
I will be triumphant
I will be victorious
This is a battle I will win
I am powerful

DAY 190

Let the flames of your faith consume your fears

. . .

Be determined to live a life full of joy, peace, purpose and passion. Every door that needs to open for you, will be open. Every form of assistance or help will be made available, every obstacle will be overcome. You are not dependent on external sources you have everything you need and put your mind to. Your faith is a fire within you, ignite it and let it burn brightly, let it consume the lies of fear that you cannot make it or that you are not good enough. Your faith validates you, because it gives you the energy to do whatever it takes to make what you want to do a reality. Your faith silences fear, it allows you to rise above it and soar. Feed your faith, allow it to constantly grow. It will serve you well and take you to places you can only imagine.

MY DAILY WOW AFFIRMATION

I have faith I will succeed
I live a life of purpose
I live a life of peace
I am confident I will make it
I am confident I will win

DAY 191

Anything that leaves your life is preparing room for something much better

. . .

Things and people come and go for a season and for a reason, be at peace with walking in wholeness and completion within yourself when that happens. The absence of something only means the space of something even better exists, to welcome the new. Don't feel like you lack anything, or like you are deficient. With or without certain things or people in your life, you still have everything you need for where you are now. And whatever else you are in need of will come. Make room for more. Empty yourself of the old in preparation for what is to come. Expand yourself to create even more room and to enlarge your capacity for more. You will not be without if you have a need, it will be met for the purpose of you being complete and whole, needing and requiring nothing.

MY DAILY WOW AFFIRMATION

Room is being created for me
Better things are coming into my life
Negativity is leaving my life
What is not for me is leaving me
I am preparing to receive great things

DAY 192

Be grateful for what you have now and hopeful for what you want in the future

. . .

Gratefulness prepares room for more and better things. Adopt an attitude of gratitude. Be grateful and thankful for what you have and who you are. Appreciate how far you have come on your journey, the people around you and the help you have received. In being grateful, it is ok to desire more. You can be hopeful for better things and more than what you have now. Desiring more does not discount your gratitude. You can be grateful and hopeful simultaneously. You can always appreciate how far you've come on a journey; it doesn't mean you want to stay there or that the journey is over, it is ok to want to finish the course and complete the race as you should. But having gratitude is understanding the importance of the effort involved in you getting to the place where you are now.

MY DAILY WOW AFFIRMATION

I am grateful for my blessings
I am hopeful for better things to come
I am expectant of greatness
I am thankful of how far I've come
I will finish my journey successfully

DAY 193

There is nothing that is impossible if you believe

. . .

There are so many things that have been done in history that was once impossible, however someone's crazy belief in the possibility of the impossible is what you are enjoying today. It was once impossible to fly, now there are aircrafts that carry over 500 people in the sky daily. It was once impossible to communicate with people that were not in close proximity to you, now you can see and speak to people all around the world at any time of the day. It was once impossible to capture and relive a moment in time exactly how it was experienced, now you can record and share experiences with anyone and everyone you choose to in a video. What are you hoping for? What would you like to see in the world that does not currently exist? All you need to do is believe.

MY DAILY WOW AFFIRMATION

I will achieve the impossible
I believe in my ability
I have divine favour
I attract good things into my life
I welcome awesome opportunities

DAY 194

One day you will thank yourself for never giving up

. . .

You won't regret trying, especially if trying leads to great success. What you will regret are the opportunities you never took because you were too afraid or too busy doing something you won't even remember. The effort that you make towards achieving something is never wasted. Keep going no matter what, you won't regret it. Keep challenging yourself to be a more refined version of yourself. One thing is sure is that time will pass. What you want to achieve in that time is completely up to you. But whatever you want to achieve will require work, discipline and self-control, all of which you have, you will only be required to exercise it. But it will be worth it if you do, you will be thankful that you did and so will everyone that benefits from your diligence in remaining consistent and not giving up.

MY DAILY WOW AFFIRMATION

I will not give up
I will not give in
I will not lose hope
I have faith I will make it
I will achieve great things

DAY 195

They may see you struggle but don't let them ever see you quit

. . .

People are constantly watching and waiting to see how you respond to what life throws at you. They await your response frequently. Don't feel ashamed at your situation during the times things are not at their best. You are human and you are dealing with real life problems. There is no point of trying to glamourize your struggle because the truth will always come out in the end. In fact, let them watch how you navigate through challenging situations. But one thing you can never do is quit. No matter how hard it gets and how weak you feel. Do not surrender to your feelings of defeat. Rise, each time you fall and slip, get right back up again. You are not a failure. Even if you fail you keep trying until you succeed. Let that be what they see. Be determined to not give up.

MY DAILY WOW AFFIRMATION

I will not fall
I will rise
I will not crumble under pressure
I will become stronger
I will overcome

DAY 196

Align yourself with your divine purpose

. . .

Know what you want out of life and know what life wants out of you. To live a fulfilling meaningful life, you need to align the two. What do you want to achieve? What makes you happy? What are you passionate about? What can you do more of? What can you do to improve life for those around you? Take time to think about the importance of not just wanting to increase your value, but to bring value in everything you do. How can the skills you have acquired be used to serve something greater than yourself? How can you give back with no obvious reward for yourself? Life is so much better when you are able to give to others with no expectation that you will receive anything back from them. The rewards you receive are things that can be taken for granted, like spending time with the people you care about most.

MY DAILY WOW AFFIRMATION

I am walking in divine purpose
I am making the right decisions
I am walking through the right doors
I am connecting with the right people
I am surrounded with like-minded people

DAY 197

Stay patient and trust that everything will work itself out

. . .

There will be times you just have to wait. In your waiting remain active. This is not a time to be passive or complacent. Instead keep doing the work that is required of you to achieve your goals, don't stop, remain focused, stay consistent. Trust time to bring you what you desire of it the most. Have faith that what you are working towards will take shape and fall into place like you are expecting it to. Something will happen, it is just a matter of time. Let the time pass and remain faithfully patient. Don't watch the clock, or sit around looking at the time go by, instead stay active and busy focusing on what you need to do in this time to prepare for what it is that you want. Be ready for it to come at any time.

MY DAILY WOW AFFIRMATION

I will remain patient
I will trust my journey
Everything is working out for me
I will stay focused
I will keep my eye on the prize

DAY 198

Know yourself

· · ·

The journey of self is the most beautiful and rewarding journey you will ever take. Don't be afraid of what you might find along the way, the beauty is in where it will take you. Spend time with you, getting to know who you are, what you like, what makes you tick, what gets you upset. What makes you excited. Being self-aware will serve you well because it will make you understand your power and use it to propel you forward. It will also give you confidence to withstand people that will try to control and manipulate you. Invest in yourself via self-care. Reserve time for you to rest and recuperate, for you to indulge in leisure activities, for you to do things that excite you and take you out of your comfort zone. This will make you a happier, stronger more balanced version of yourself.

MY DAILY WOW AFFIRMATION

I am learning what is best for me
I am becoming more self-aware
I am making decisions that serve my purpose
I am expectant of the reward at the end
I am understanding and using my strengths

DAY 199

External appearances, in the absence of a deep warm soul is merely superficial

. . .

Work on the beauty within so your external beauty will show through and won't be just a cover up of your internal turmoil. The thing about a mask is that it is evidence of fakery, it is either too perfect or does not vary. Real emotions are sensitive to its surroundings and to show it you must understand this. Your act of kindness today may not have the same impact tomorrow as it did today, so take into account the needs of the recipient. What do they need from you? Is it a loving gesture? A smile a word of encouragement? Is it financial assistance? Or some sort of helping hand? Whatever it is, do it with an intentional heart to bring genuine joy to the person you are doing it for. This reveals the authenticity of your internal beauty.

MY DAILY WOW AFFIRMATION

I am working on my internal beauty
I am investing on my internal state
I am working on being whole within myself
I am pursuing completion
I am working on being my best

DAY 200

It may be hard, but hard does not mean impossible

. . .

If it can be done, you can do it. Though it may be hard, you are tough enough to get it done; step by step, one day at a time. And even if you fall, you will rise up again, when you fail, you will learn from your mistakes and try again. You will push through until you get it. For it is not impossible to accomplish what it is that you want to do. It may be hard, but you are tough. It may be difficult, but it is not impossible. Do what you need to do, to get it done. Get the help, ask for assistance if necessary. You can and you will make it. You've done it before to get this far and you can keep doing it to get further and further until you reach your desired destination. Keep the prize in sight.

MY DAILY WOW AFFIRMATION

My goals are not impossible
I have the power to make my dreams happen
I believe I can reach my goals
I am confident I have all I need within me
Anything I lack that I need will come into my life

DAY 201

The private conversations will happen regardless, keep shining

. . .

There will always be someone that has something to say about you, give them something exciting to talk about. Make your life interesting, let it take unexpected turns and twists. Do not be predictable, surprise them. Remain gracious and honest. Let your hard work and results speak for themselves. Don't be afraid to celebrate your achievements, you have worked hard and deserve all your accolades. Be daring and exciting, take unexpected risks. Stretch yourself, do more than you think you can do. Challenge yourself and prove yourself that you can. Step out of your comfort zone, do something outside of the box. Be colourful and brave. Be calm and collected. Do not feel the need to defend or justify yourself. Your truth will resound louder than any lie. Most importantly be true to you, don't conform to anyone else's standards, you are good enough and more than enough.

MY DAILY WOW AFFIRMATION

I will not focus on external opinions
I will not be distracted by naysayers
I will continue to shine my light
I will keep my fire burning
I will remain passionate

DAY 202

Programme your mind for success

. . .

Renew your mind, and get it fixed on being successful no matter what. Clear your mind from failure or the thought that it cannot work. Remove doubt or fear. Fill yourself with positive prospects. Read testimonials and examples of people that have made it despite adversity. Make an active choice that no matter what you will make it, you will not give up. See the task as can be done and not can't be done, see the solution not the problem. Do not entertain the thought of giving up. Let your faith rise above the doubt. See success, see yourself as already achieving and making it. Use your past successes as a foundation to stand on, you have been successful in something you haven't done before, but you did it and became good at it and you can do it again.

MY DAILY WOW AFFIRMATION

I will programme my mind for success
I will stay optimistic
I will cultivate a good attitude
I will continue to have faith
I will believe in my achievement

DAY 203

Turn your excuses into execution

. . .

Excuses bear no weight, they bear no added value and can be a hindrance. Instead of giving excuses, show a willingness to act. Stop saying you are not going to do it because it won't work. Try and do it again because this time, it will work. Stop saying you don't have time, start prioritising your time, so that you can do what you need to do. Stop saying that someone like you has never done it before. There are numerous amounts of people that are the first to ever do what hasn't been done before. Be the first. Turn your reason for not doing it to the reason why you must. You must do it because no one like you ever has, you must do it because time is limited, you must do it because up until this point it hasn't worked and you therefore must find a way to make it work.

MY DAILY WOW AFFIRMATION

I will execute my plans
I will not give excuses
I will apply action to my faith
I will prioritise my goals
I will do whatever it takes

DAY 204

You are capable, brave and significant

. . .

Lift your head up, fight on, be brave and strong. Even if it feels like it's a lost cause, keep going like you are sure of the win. Because in the end you will surely win. It can be done and you will be the one to do it. You lack nothing that you need, you have everything you need as it is already inside of you, your gift and purpose are woven into your DNA, your existence makes you valid for this task at hand. You are already special and there is nothing that you need in addition, to be more worthy. You are brave and strong, you have come this far despite your fear and doubt because deep down you know it is possible. You have nothing to lose. You are important and significant, you don't have to come from a reputable family, you are complete and entire within yourself.

MY DAILY WOW AFFIRMATION

I am capable
I am brave
I am significant
I have a divine skill
I have a unique ability

DAY 205

Your faith can move mountains but fear can create them

. . .

Don't create limitations, hurdles and boundaries with your doubt. Rather, use your faith to push through, breakthrough and jump through. Your faith removes the obstacle, it makes the obstacle insignificant in comparison to where you are going. The limitation is a mere hump in the road in comparison to where you need to go. Your faith has the power to remove hindrances and make them non-existent. However, when you entertain doubt it creates mountains that never existed, it stops you and holds you back. Don't let doubt in, don't let it imprison you. Fear is a liar. Silence it and rise above it. Use faith to bring down; everything that will try to get in your way and stop you from moving forward and everything that will fill you with fear and overwhelm you.

MY DAILY WOW AFFIRMATION

I am moving mountains with my faith
I will rise above every doubt
I am not letting my doubt limit me
I am removing hindrances from my life
I refuse to give into fear

DAY 206

Failure is just your first attempt in learning

. . .

Fail fast and fail often. Don't miss an opportunity to learn and grow. Failure is not a bad thing, it is an important part of success and making it in life. Failure is part of your journey. Failure is critical for your growth; it shapes who you are and who you will be. Do not fear the effects of failure. It will not destroy you, it will only act as a stepping stone for your progression. Keep trying and failing, and while you fail, observe the lesson. Use the knowledge that you have gained from failing, in your next attempt. Can you see progression? Over time you will get better until you are the very best. Be obsessed with learning and getting better. Do not focus on failing, focus on winning, focus on getting better on your next attempt. As you do this you will get closer to your goal until you eventually win.

MY DAILY WOW AFFIRMATION

I will learn from my failures
I am committed to my journey
I am determined to succeed
I will keep going until I succeed
I will not let temporary failure hold me back

DAY 207

What has been written about you so far cannot compare to how the story ends

. . .

Keep writing, creating, growing, evolving. Your story isn't over until you win. And you win by consistency every day, showing up and showing out. You win by not giving up. You win by moving forward even when you are tired and feel like you haven't got a clue what you are doing. You win by standing strong when the storms of life wage against you. Keep winning every day. Don't stop, don't look back. Progress and move forward. It doesn't matter how and where you started. What is important is where you are now and where you are heading towards. You are the author of your life, how do you want the story to end? What do you want to do next? What lives do you want to change for the better? Focus your energy on making the end of your story the best ending it can be.

MY DAILY WOW AFFIRMATION

I will make sure my story ends well
I will change my story for the better
I am growing
I am evolving
I am becoming more consistent day by day

DAY 208

...and at that point God steps in

· · ·

Just be reassured that God is on the matter. Hold your head high and believe that God has everything under control. It's hard to be in a place where you feel like you have absolutely no grip on life, which direction you are going in, what will be your fate. But don't worry about these things, as fear and worry deplete your energy, weaken you and cloud your judgement. Rather trust and hope in a power greater than your own, a power that wants you to win and wants the best for your life. When there is nothing left for you to do and you have done all you can, trust that God will work things out for you, that the matter will be settled in your favour. Do not fear the worse, but trust and expect the best possible outcome for you to happen.

MY DAILY WOW AFFIRMATION

I trust God will turn things around in my favour
The way will be made clear
I will not worry
I will be at peace
I will trust that everything will work out

DAY 209

Don't be complacent, complacency kills progression

. . .

When you are doing well and everything is going smoothly, it is easy to get complacent. However, complacency is an enemy of growth. When you see yourself getting too relaxed and you do not feel like you are being challenged, this is a time that you need to get out of your comfort zone. It is time to take it up a gear and speed progression. It is a time where you can expand yourself to take on more. Stretch yourself, enlarge your capacity for greater. Greatness is not built in your comfort zone. Playing it safe over a long period of time means a very slow and long drawn out progression, if any at all. Why go slow when you can do more? And in doing more you get to your destination quicker. Therefore, use time more effectively so that your impact and reach is greater.

MY DAILY WOW AFFIRMATION

I will not get complacent
I will remain focused
I will stretch myself to accelerate
I will expand my reach
I will be committed to progress

DAY 210

Be the hero you once needed to rescue you

. . .

If you are still waiting on someone to rescue you, you may be waiting your whole life. Use whatever resources you have as fuel to get you to where you want to go. Reach out and save yourself from going to that place of no return, a place of sorrow and deep regret. Save yourself from yourself, if you realise you can be your worse enemy, when you entertain doubt or feelings of worthlessness. What you are looking for externally, find internally. Be your own Hero. You are capable of doing more than anyone else could possibly do for you. If you take the time to invest in yourself and your skills, you can get yourself out of any situation that appears to be unfavourable, by finding a solution. Be solution orientated and not problem focused. Your freedom is in your faith to believe you can rise.

MY DAILY WOW AFFIRMATION

I have the power to improve my situation
I have all the resources I need within me
I am capable of amazing things
I will invest in improving my skills
My faith liberates me

DAY 211

Fall in love with yourself and who you are becoming

. . .

How people feel towards you is insignificant in comparison to how you feel towards yourself. The whole world could love you, but if you hate yourself, you are a prisoner of your self-hatred. It limits you and prevents you from seeing the beauty in a situation. It makes you ungrateful for what you have and only focus on what you lack. Learn to first like yourself and what you do and then to love who you are. If you don't like yourself, consider the reasons why and then work on changing these things. Become the person who you would like to be and the way you would like to look. Work on yourself to become your best self. Be a version of yourself that will make you proud, a version of yourself that you love and want to be. Doing this makes life more exciting and worth living.

MY DAILY WOW AFFIRMATION

I am becoming someone great
I am becoming a better version of myself
I love who I am becoming
I am improving daily
I am making positive steps towards change

DAY 212

You can change at any point in time

. . .

If things are not working the way you would like. You don't have to suffer in silence, you can do something to change your situation. If you are in a place that is not conducive for your growth, change location. Don't feel like you are stuck in doing it one way or in one particular place. At any given time, you can change. You can change your surroundings, you can change your direction, you can change your career, you can change your style. Only because this is the way that most people identify you, it doesn't mean that you can't do things differently. You are still you and the essence of who you are is the same, but you want to grow and develop, and in order to do this, something has to change. Change by making a decision followed by action and then commit to seeing the changes through.

MY DAILY WOW AFFIRMATION

I am changing for the better
I am surrounding myself with positivity
I am cultivating a growth mind-set
I am building habits conducive for my development
I am making beneficial decisions

DAY 213

Do it because making yourself proud is what matters most

. . .

Don't try and impress the whole world and then end up feeling miserable. Make sure you do it for yourself and that you get results that you are happy with. There are so many people to get inspiration from and who you can do things for. It could be your parents, your spouse or your kids and although these are all very worthy reasons to want to succeed, it is important to want to succeed for yourself too. If making them happy, makes you happy then even better. But if all you are doing is to make someone else happy, you can end up feeling unfulfilled and empty. After accomplishing something great, feeling unfulfilled can be one of the worst things you can experience. Make sure in everything you do, you are fulfilling your own happiness and making yourself proud too.

MY DAILY WOW AFFIRMATION

I will complete my journey
I will make myself proud
I am fighting a worthy cause
I will accomplish greatness
I am fulfilling destiny

DAY 214

Your life gets better by change not by chance

. . .

You have to be intentional about what you want from life. You are not successful by coincidence, it is something you have to work towards and strive for. You have to make the necessary changes to see positive and permanent transformation. If you want to create a happy life, a life you are proud of, there are specific steps you have to take and moves you have to make, you can't be casual about your progression in life. You honestly need to think about what actions you need to take, who you need to get in contact with, how you can get help to take on big projects and what investments you need to put in, to see your projects are completed. If you want to live a superior life and not a life of mediocrity make the required changes now.

MY DAILY WOW AFFIRMATION

My life is changing for the better
I am making continuous improvement
I am making positive changes
I am dedicated to growth
I am working towards permanent transformation

DAY 215

Life starts feeling like a blessing when you acknowledge it is one

. . .

When you realise how blessed you are, you open yourself up for more blessings. Doors of opportunity and success begin to locate you, the path that leads to your desired destination, become easier to navigate and is made straight, so you are less likely to derail. Your gratitude for the blessings, big and small allow for you to obtain strength from a source greater than you. Through gratitude you receive a new measure of this strength to overcome any obstacle or challenge that poses a threat to you. You are empowered for your journey and people and situations favour you. Acknowledging your blessings and being grateful for them gives you a sense of joy and energy to face any trial that comes your way, it increases your confidence, gives you peace and allows you to find rest in the midst of unsettling situations. Treat life like a blessing and you will be blessed.

MY DAILY WOW AFFIRMATION

I am blessed
I am grateful for life
I am thankful for every good thing in my life
I continue to attract more blessings
I will get to my desired destination

DAY 216

Don't let anyone determine your value, when they do not know your worth

. . .

Know who are. Knowing your worth changes the course of your life, it puts you in places you can only dream of or imagine. Do not let anyone undermine you or make you feel less than who you are. You are amazing and capable of wonderful things. Anyone who says and thinks otherwise is a liar, they are just reflecting their own insecurities onto you. Do not receive the hurtful lies they say or the disturbing way they try to make you feel. Know within yourself how powerful and precious you are. Let your confidence in who you are and the reason you were created radiate in all you do. You were created for a reason and at the right time. You are special and you are a masterpiece. You are unique, exclusive and rare, your value is without measure. And only because someone can't see it doesn't mean it isn't so.

MY DAILY WOW AFFIRMATION

I am precious
I am valuable
I do not need external validation
I am amazing
I am awesome

DAY 217

Quit quitting and start becoming who you were born to be

. . .

It's time to put a stop to giving up. It hasn't worked for you and it never will. Giving up is designed to hold you back and stop you from achieving the great and wonderful things you were designed to do. Have who you want to be and what you want to achieve fixed in your mind. Let it be a very vivid picture, to a level where it is so tangible you can almost touch, feel and sense you are already in that place. But you will not get there anytime soon if you keep giving yourself allowances. When you feel like giving up, look at that picture, experience how it feels to stand in those future shoes and have that great sense of accomplishment. Now remember that the challenge you are in now will be over shortly if you just continue and do not stop.

MY DAILY WOW AFFIRMATION

I will not quit

I am not a quitter

I will not stop until I achieve my goals

I will accomplish every goal

I am capable of wonderful things

DAY 218

Stop sharing your vision with the wrong people

. . .

Although people may love and care for you, they may not always understand why you do what you do and because of it they may question your reasons for pursuing your goals or try to discourage you in one way or another. Do not be angry or upset with them, they may be coming from a genuine place, but they are limited in their perspective and perception, therefore any advice they give will be warped. Do not disclose your dreams and visions with them as they will not protect and nurture it like you will and can actually end up causing serious damage. Stay true to yourself and keep your light shining. In time all will be revealed to the appropriate people. Remain a person of integrity whose opinion can be respected even if people do not agree with you all the time.

MY DAILY WOW AFFIRMATION

I will protect my vision
I will invest in my vision
I will not expose my vision to the wrong people
I believe in my vision
I know I will make it

DAY 219

Nobody can stop what God is about to do in your life

· · ·

Whether the people around you like you or not. They cannot stop what has been ordained for you before you were even formed and emerged in this world. Whether they know you or not. They cannot stop God's hand or favour on your life. The beauty about God is that the blessings distributed from heaven are not just for the most deserving, they are completely independent of what you have or have not done. So, no one has the right to dictate if you are worthy or unworthy of the wonderful things that are happening in your life. Rest assured what you have cannot be taken away and if it is, it is only temporary. Everything that is for you will be restored to you. When you step out in boldness and faith, let nature take its course and God come through for you at the perfect time.

MY DAILY WOW AFFIRMATION

I cannot be stopped
God will do amazing things in my life
Nobody can stop my blessings
Everything that is meant for me will find me
Everything will happen when the time is right

DAY 220

Winners never quit

. . .

Quitters don't win and winners do not quit. So to win you have to stay in the race. Finish what you start. Do not quit under any circumstances. It is not always the fastest people that win the race, but the ones who can stay the full length of the course and see it through to the end. Finish what you start, do not give up along the way no matter how difficult it gets, you are strong enough to see it through until the end. You have what it takes to overcome and finish strong, you have everything in you to win, so keep on going. Don't stop, even if you have to go at a slower pace, it is ok to slow down, but it is not ok to stop, it is not ok to give up and quit.

Make yourself proud, you haven't come this far to lose.

MY DAILY WOW AFFIRMATION

I am a winner

I will not quit

I will not stop

I will continue moving forward until I reach my goal

I will finish strong

DAY 221

Success is a series of small wins

. . .

Focus on the small wins that lead to big victories. You don't always have to come first in the race to win, consistently beating your personal best is a win. You may not see an increase in the number of clients you have just yet, but consistently building a better brand that sells a high quality product or service is a win. You may not lose the desired weight you were intending on, but getting stronger and becoming more disciplined is still a win. These small victories lead to you winning constantly and eventually winning big. The key thing is to remain consistent. Even if you do not see the results you were expecting, continuing on the track you are on will see you winning regardless.

MY DAILY WOW AFFIRMATION

I am winning
I will have many wins
I am taking each goal step by step
I will continue to succeed
I will continue to be victorious

DAY 222

True beauty is accepting yourself for who you are

. . .

There's something completely liberating about accepting the skin you are in. Walking your own walk and living your own life, at your own pace, gives you peace of mind. You are living for yourself on your clock, not by how society tells you to live or when and what you should accomplish in life. Many people only share the story of their glory and not the battle they faced to get there. Appreciate your journey and stay in your own lane. If this does not work for you it is ok to switch things up and change lanes. It is completely up to you. Be who you want to be and enjoy being that, that is true beauty and success in its own right.

MY DAILY WOW AFFIRMATION

I accept myself for who I am
I am learning to love myself daily
I embrace my development
I appreciate my journey
I am constantly growing

DAY 223

No matter how many times you fall, stand back up

. . .

They can try to bring you down, but they cannot keep you down. You are engineered to succeed. Your mind is renewed, your confession is positive, your actions from now are setting you up for an expected end and that is to win. You will win; everything you have been fighting for up until this point is so that you can win. You have built muscle along the way so that you have strength to see this through to the end. You are victorious and you can take on any challenge and conquer any mountain. You are brave and brilliant, you are wise and humble. Even though you may fall you will rise and you will keep on rising no matter the situation. Although the storm may rage, you will make it through. Continue to stand strong, you were born for this.

MY DAILY WOW AFFIRMATION

I will get back up when I fall
I will continue to stand firm
I will keep going
I won't be fazed or taken off course
I will continue to be brave

DAY 224

It is never too late to be what you might have been

. . .

It does not matter where, how or when you start. What matters is that you start and it is important to start now, from where you are, with what you have. It is not too late. No matter when you start, you can start that business, complete that qualification, write the content for that project, change career, start building that house. You have an advantage of experience that is rich and detailed, you can bring your wealth of knowledge from the school of life into this new venture. Even if you are a novice you can reach out to the many people you have met along the way who will be happy to help you. Many people have started something new at a time that is uncommon to pursue it, but they have been extremely successful because they believed in their ability to succeed. You can do same and more.

MY DAILY WOW AFFIRMATION

My blessings will arrive right on time

I will start now

I will not delay

My time is coming

I will trust my process

DAY 225

Even if everything around you crumbles you will not

. . .

Sometimes it can feel like your whole world is falling apart. And even if it is, just know that you will survive. Even if the world turns it's back on you, you will get through it. The worst thing that you could ever imagine could somehow be your fate today, know that it will not last forever and that you will make it through. The loss of a loved one, a job or a home, can make you feel completely displaced. But know that although the pain is unbearable and you wish you didn't have to go through this, you will make it out on the other side, stronger. You have been designed and engineered to face every battle and challenge that comes your way, it will not be able to destroy you. You are stronger than you think, braver than you know, more powerful than you can ever imagine.

MY DAILY WOW AFFIRMATION

I will not be shaken
I will not be moved
I will not give up
I will not stop
I will keep on going

DAY 226

You are blessed because you believe

. . .

How wonderful is it to have exactly what you believed in, come to pass. And the truth of the matter is, you are more likely to have what you desire, come to pass because of your faith. Believing, surrounds you with energy and connects you with the right people, it allows you to see opportunities that you may have not recognised before. Faith gives you boldness to ask for things and the confidence that you will get it. You are more fortunate when you take a step of faith and believe in your vision, goal and aspiration. Doubt robs you of your joy and hinders you from taking a chance on opportunities that can bring you closer to your goal. Do not allow doubt to stop you reaching for what could be yours, believe and hope for what you want to come true.

MY DAILY WOW AFFIRMATION

I am blessed
My faith attracts more blessings
I believe my breakthrough is coming
I will achieve my goals
I am closer to my destination

DAY 227

See the perfection in time

. . .

Opportunities may seem like they are taking forever to arrive. It may feel like everyone's time has come and you are last on the list. Remain diligent and do not lose sight of the goal. Your time will come when you have learnt all that you need to know in order to be able to receive this new level of responsibility. Everything that appears out of your control God is aligning in your favour. Be active and intentional over the things you have control over, do not procrastinate or shift the responsibility to others. Use your God-given power and ability to do all you can with all you have. For when your time comes you will need to be ready to operate in your most effective state of mind. Start preparing for the results you want to see, so that when it happens you can make the most of the opportunity.

MY DAILY WOW AFFIRMATION

Everything will happen in perfect timing
I wait patiently for my blessings
I do not get discouraged by delay
I do not get distracted during the wait
My time is coming

DAY 228

You have been given this life because you are strong enough to live it

. . .

Even when you do not feel like it, you are stronger than you could ever imagine. Your strength is further refined when you are at your weakest. That pain that you are going through, the pressure that you are facing, the never-ending struggle is all part of building your mental muscle and your capacity for more However during this time, do not be afraid to reach out for help. It is ok to be vulnerable. It is totally normal to not have all the answers or the strength to complete every task at hand. This doesn't count you out of the race or discount you from being relevant or worthy. In fact, it is because you are worthy that life has presented this challenge for you to overcome. Life has entrusted you with this life lesson as an example for others and to teach others.

So, believe you can and you will.

MY DAILY WOW AFFIRMATION

I am grateful for life
I do not take life for granted
I am thankful for my many blessings
I will cope when I face conflict
I will use my strength when I am under pressure

DAY 229

In the rain look for rainbows, in the dark of the night look for stars

. . .

When life presents challenges and it appears that all hope is loss. Know that hope is never lost. There is always hope. But you have to make a conscious decision to see it. You have to unlock a perspective that is only accessible to those that earnestly search for it, with the expectation that you will receive exactly what you see in your mind. And because of this vision; your faith will increase, therefore making the vision clearer. Furthermore, opportunities will miraculously appear in order to make your vision a reality, because you are conscious of what will be, you are able to reach out and access what you need to. This doesn't mean anything in life is easy, however it is easier when you see the positive possibilities that have always been there, you just had to focus on them as opposed to the negativity.

MY DAILY WOW AFFIRMATION

I have a positive outlook on life
I am optimistic
My spirit is lifted
I am joyful
I cultivate peace

DAY 230

Be as happy as you choose to be

. . .

Only because everyone around you is miserable, you don't have to be miserable. Especially because you have so many things to be grateful for. And your gratitude opens up more room for you to receive, because you know how to appreciate good things; more good things will come your way. It is totally understandable to be sensitive to the feelings of others especially when they are going through really difficult times in their lives. However, instead of being brought down by their low mood, use your light within to be a source of joy, peace and hope. Lift and shift their negativity and darkness to positivity and light. Don't take on and be weighed down by their problems, rather encourage them with possible solutions. And if you cannot help them, that is ok, their burdens are not for you to carry. You have to run and win your own race.

MY DAILY WOW AFFIRMATION

I choose to be happy
My happiness is not dependent on external factors
I am grateful for the good things in my life
I do not let discouragement overwhelm me
My light gives me hope

DAY 231

Your best is still to come

. . .

Better things are coming. Wait on it, don't give up too soon. Even if you are operating at your optimum and things seem to be going well. Enjoy and appreciate the moment, but never get comfortable. You have capacity for more. Master the level that you are on with the expectation that as you desire more, more will come. Better things will develop as you remain consistent. The universe is ever expanding and there are no limits, so keep that in mind, that there are even greater things that await you, your best now can and will be better. Keep pushing, keep the momentum, do not settle. There is no limit to your reach or what you can do. Continue to desire the best and the best will make itself available to you. It is possible to be satisfied with what you have and still desire greater, having peace that it will come.

MY DAILY WOW AFFIRMATION

The best is yet to come
I will not give up
I will not get distracted
My expectations are being met
My desires are coming to pass

DAY 232

Small steps in the right direction can be the most significant steps of your life

· · ·

Never despise small changes no matter how insignificant they feel. These changes accumulated make the most significant impact in your life. The most important thing is to remain consistent. Keep moving, keep changing, keep gaining ground. Every effort is relevant. Every movement forward is important. It is hard at times to even see that anything has materialised or anything has changed when you have put the work in, but continue whether you can see the change or not, because like a miracle those changes will start to show and will make a significance in your life. You are becoming more disciplined, patient, persistent in the process, which are all virtues that you require to become the best version of yourself. Keep making steps towards your goal and do not look back you are getting closer to your destination, it doesn't matter how fast or slow you go, just keep moving.

MY DAILY WOW AFFIRMATION

I am stepping in the right direction
I am taking one step at a time
My efforts are relevant
I am walking by faith
I will keep moving forward

DAY 233

What you were yesterday does not define who you are today

. . .

You are constantly changing day by day. Do not let who you were yesterday discourage the person you can be today. Even if people remind you of the mistakes you made in the past. That is who you were. You have a choice right now to change. You do not have to be stuck in being or doing things a certain way, just because that is how other people identify you. You can determine who you want to be by being that person right now. It may take some time for you to completely change, but you can start the process. It may require you making some very drastic external changes, and even changing location. But the most important change occurs internally. And once you make that decision to be more than who you once were, commit to this change until the process is complete.

MY DAILY WOW AFFIRMATION

I am getting better day by day
My past failures do not discourage me
I am constantly evolving
I am improving continuously
I am becoming more of the person I want to be

DAY 234

It rarely happens overnight

. . .

Most endeavours involve some sort of process. A start that needs work to be taken off the ground, then consistent, regular effort for progression. At times during the process what you may discover is that for some time it will appear like nothing is happening and that the work is not yielding any outcome, however this requires you to still keep putting in the work. You may have to put in even more effort, or completely change your method for a different stage within the same process. This can occur in cycles and can leave you feeling drained, however do not stop or give up, because if you do, you sometimes, have to start the whole process again. It may take time, but don't lose sight of the end, keep going, the day and time will come when all the hard work and effort will pay off.

MY DAILY WOW AFFIRMATION

I am aware that good things take time
My diligence will pay off
I will see the rewards in due time
I will commit to the hard work
I will continue to make an effort

DAY 235

Live a life worthy of the person that you are aspiring to be

. . .

You are self-sufficient and have everything in you that is needed to be great. You do not have to convince yourself of something that you already have or that you already are. You simply have to unlock it. You have to search within. You have to take the time to look inwards and see yourself for who you truly are. You are marvellous, you are a piece of the most divine artwork, carefully woven and knit into a living and breathing, intelligent powerhouse, that is capable of remarkable things. Dare to take a chance on yourself. Dare to not just dream, but make that dream a reality. If it can be done, why not you? Why can't you be the first that has ever achieved what you want to achieve, under the circumstances that you are attempting to achieve it? It can be done, and you can be the one to do it.

MY DAILY WOW AFFIRMATION

I am marvellous
I am a masterpiece
I am working towards who I want to be
I am taking each day as it comes
My efforts are effective

DAY 236

Have faith and a plan, that's how you really win in life.

. . .

You may have a plan without the faith to see it through, you may find yourself swayed from or discouraged about completing your journey. The importance of being strategic, is by planning out a method of which you will acquire what it is that you hope for, shines a light on your path. Your goals will not happen on just a wish and a prayer, it involves work, action, commitment and intention. Faith and action work hand in hand. If you really want to be successful. You have to know and believe that your plan will work. This is what keeps you going when you encounter bumps in the road, or when the storms of life hit against the sails guiding you, remember you can steer the sail and use the wind to go in the direction of your destination, this is how faith works, it keeps you on track.

MY DAILY WOW AFFIRMATION

My faith creates action
I make strategic decisions
I am in control of the direction of my life
I am powerful
I am executing my plans

DAY 237

Know what you want and do not settle for less

. . .

To go for your desires may not be an easy task, however it is very fulfilling and rewarding. Settling will often diminish your self-worth and value. You are worthy of great and amazing things. It is not self-indulgent to want more or the very best, it is your right. You have the right to want the best for yourself. Give your best and demand your best back. Never devalue yourself to appease anyone or to appear humble. Humility is not settling for the least; it is knowing and appreciating your worth, but not lauding it over anyone else. You can be humble and still give and require the best for yourself. Do not settle. Keep striving for greatness and thriving in your pursuit for more. Do not see yourself as small, unworthy or incapable, you can and you will receive the things you set your heart upon to achieve once you believe.

MY DAILY WOW AFFIRMATION

I believe I will get what I desire
I will not settle for second best
I will strive for excellence
I will strive to be the best
I am pursuing greatness

DAY 238

It is easier to walk in a straight line once you have a fixed point to follow

. . .

Stay focused. It is easier to miss your way if your focus is not fixed on where you are going. There are so many distractions to deter you, but resist every distraction. It is only for a short while that you have to focus. So do everything within yourself to make sure you keep your eyes fixed on where you are going, so that you can get there faster. When you get to where you want to go, then you can rest or indulge in leisure. But for now, you have to work hard and give it all that you have got. Keep going, do not stop. If you need to isolate yourself then isolate yourself, if you need to be around people that are on the same journey as you then get around those people. Do whatever works for you as long as it keeps you on track.

MY DAILY WOW AFFIRMATION

I am focused
I have tunnel vision
I am intentional with my goals
My eyes are on the prize
I have my goals in sight

DAY 239

Don't give up, the beginning can always seem like the hardest

. . .

It can be easy to want to put off something that you know involves your full effort, focus and determination, with no guarantee that it will yield the results you even want. Do not be deterred. Just start, no matter how small and no matter how slowly you go. Do whatever is necessary to get the ball rolling. Make the call, send the email, start writing, start producing, pick up the paint brush, book that ticket, get in the car, knock on that door, take the first step and keep walking until you are strong enough to run. Because what you will find is once you get started things, will take off and you will find a rhythm that will keep you going. And if you don't find it the first time, keep starting until you do find it. It's ok to start more than once. There are no rules for getting it done. Just get it done.

MY DAILY WOW AFFIRMATION

I will not be overwhelmed
I will not give up
I will keep on going
I will push through
I am resilient

DAY 240

Be still

. . .

At times you will find that the best thing to do, is to do nothing. Be silent, be still, stay calm; in the midst of chaos and disorder when the situation requires you to act and to act fast, but you have no idea of what to do. Don't act in haste and be reactive, as you could make a costly decision; rather than this, shut out the noise and take the time to think things through. Be intentional, you are required to be responsible for your actions, that may impact the course of your life and that of others. This situation demands that you make a decision that is well thought through. Do not use it as an excuse to procrastinate or worry about getting things wrong. Get in-tune with yourself, away from your surroundings and own all of your thoughts and actions.

MY DAILY WOW AFFIRMATION

I will not fret
I will not fear
I am calm
I am at peace
I am in control of my actions

DAY 241

Work hard and keep humble

. . .

Work hard and as you do, remain humble. You never know who you will meet along your journey and who you may need assistance from. People are more willing to support you, if they know you are willing to be helped. Be kind, it doesn't cost you anything in addition to your daily living expenses. Smile and whatever you do, do with a cheerful heart, it attracts open doors. Be loyal, your reputation and integrity are far greater than temporary popularity. When all have forgotten your fame, it is the people that you have built trust with that will remember you and will be consistent with how they treat you. Be honest yet respectful, even if it makes you feel uncomfortable, you will be respected and known as trustworthy. Always be willing to learn and to teach. In learning you gain knowledge in teaching you gain understanding.

MY DAILY WOW AFFIRMATION

I am not prideful
I do not gloat
I am humble
I am grateful for my many gifts
I am thankful for life

DAY 242

The best is yet to come

. . .

While you wait get prepared. Get ready for the doors to open, opportunities to present themselves, to be elevated and celebrated for your diligence and hard work. They may have overlooked you, but don't disregard yourself, discount yourself or lose hope, the best is yet to come and in fact is coming soon. Remain humble, remain faithful and remain true to yourself. You do not need to explain yourself, you do not need to announce your next move, just wait for it. While you wait, be thankful and show your gratitude by giving. By giving, you create room to receive more. Keep working hard, keep pressing, keep pushing, don't lose sight of the prize or your goals. Celebrate your past successes and acknowledge all the work you've put in to make it this far. Your consistency will pay off and will yield a result better than your expectations.

MY DAILY WOW AFFIRMATION

My hard work will be crowned with success
I will reap the rewards of my diligence
I am preparing for more
I welcome better things to enter my life
The best is making its way to me

DAY 243

Be who you are, but aspire to be better

. . .

You are an absolute masterpiece. You are beautiful and strong. You are remarkable and mysterious. Whether you feel like it or not, you are all these fantastic things and more. How you feel does not determine who and what you are. Feeling like a car in a garage is not going to make you one. It may make you identify and understand what that feels like, but it doesn't determine that you become your feelings. Therefore, know that you are a great human being created by the highest intelligence, God the creator of all things. Know that you are created for purpose within a specific time and for a specific reason. Know that all the effort you make to add to yourself makes you more of yourself and even your mistakes and shortcomings serve their own purpose for your life. Be open to growing and always aspire to be more and do more.

MY DAILY WOW AFFIRMATION

I am using my skills
I aspire to be better
I am a work in progress
I am constantly improving
I am continuously getting better

DAY 244

Don't just learn for knowledge, learn in order for you to teach

. . .

Knowledge can be a wonderful tool to get through life's most difficult challenges. You will constantly be presented with opportunities to learn something new and expand your understanding. However, use this knowledge to enlighten and teach others. In teaching you gain understanding about what you know, that you may have not even realised or thought about before. In teaching you create a path for others and make their journey easier. In teaching you blaze a trail and give access to those, who like you desire more than what they currently possess. When you teach you bring light to someone's darkness. Teaching makes you more than who you are, by being more of what someone in need requires you to be, such as a mentor, an advisor and guide. Learning is great and even as a teacher you are constantly learning new things but never stop teaching what you know.

MY DAILY WOW AFFIRMATION

I am a teacher
I will share my knowledge
I am shining my light
I am blazing the trail
I am creating a path for others

DAY 245

Stand strong and believe in yourself

. . .

It doesn't matter who believes in you, if you don't believe in yourself you can't get to where you need to be. And it doesn't matter who doesn't believe in you, if you believe in yourself you will get to wherever you need to be. Change your posture from that of someone who has been defeated, do not be bent over, or hang your head low. Rather straighten your back, hold your head high and stand like the winner that you are. Let your confidence radiate from within. Let those that see you know, that your will, can't be broken. Let your confidence rise, because you can and you will. It may not be today or even tomorrow, but in time you will achieve what you have set out to achieve and nothing or no one will stop you. Your faith in your ability is forever growing and it will not fail you.

MY DAILY WOW AFFIRMATION

I stand strong in my beliefs
I will not waver to fit into the status quo
I will not compromise my values
I am confident in my ability to win
I will rise

DAY 246

You will never influence the world by trying to be like it

. . .

You were created unique for a reason, to leave your mark on the hearts of all those that come into contact with you. To fulfil purpose and play your part in the master plan. Don't be a carbon copy of anyone else, be your authentic self. Always remain true to yourself no matter what. Do you feel like you have lost yourself? Pause and gather your thoughts. Reflect on where and when you felt like you lost your identity and if you can't find that place, dwell on who you want to be and start there. Who do you want to be in the earth? What impact do you want to make? Whose life do you want to inspire and bless? What do you want to be remembered for and by whom? Make sure the answer to these questions will complete you, make you happy and give you peace.

MY DAILY WOW AFFIRMATION

I will use my influence for good
I will reflect purity
I will make a lasting impact
I will share hope
I will make a positive impact

DAY 247

Everything happens for a reason and for a season

. . .

Life isn't always fair. Some really bad things happen to really good people and some really good things happen to people that seem undeserving. Don't worry about the fortune of others or that of your own. Everything that happens is for a specific time and reason. Trust that your season will come and while you wait for it, get prepared. Focus on what you would like the outcome to be. Take count of how you will feel when what you earnestly want to happen, comes to pass. Don't wait for it to happen before you start to feel the excitement. Start to feel the joy of success, and a great outcome taking shape for you. Operate in your new level of responsibility. Start to perform like you are in the position you are waiting to be in. The position you are in is temporary, it's for your growth and elevation.

MY DAILY WOW AFFIRMATION

I will be content in the season I am in
I will trust the outcome will be in my favour
I will wait for change patiently
I am excited by my future
I know the story ends well

DAY 248

This too will pass

. . .

It's ok to feel disappointed, upset and frustrated. It's ok to be angry and feel cheated. It is ok to feel let down, broken and to even cry for lack of nothing else to do. But in all your feelings of rage and pain, hurt and upset do not harm others and do not harm yourself. Do not make the situation worse. Find an outlet that will not put yourself or anyone around you in danger. Your emotions are real and should not be ignored, they are true and deserve to be expressed. But don't let that expression create darkness and destruction. Let beauty and light be birthed from anguish and despair. What you are going through has a timer on it and with each second, minute, day or month, it draws closer to an end. Get the support and help you need. Do not suffer in silence and do not face it alone.

MY DAILY WOW AFFIRMATION

I will get through the storm
I will rise above the difficulty
I will overcome this challenge
The struggle is temporary
I am becoming strong through the tough times

DAY 249

Nevertheless persist

. . .

Persist and keep persisting until something happens, someone takes note and changes are made. No matter what comes your way in the form of discouragement, challenge or a closed door, keep knocking until the door is open. Keep talking about it until the right person listens, keep pressing forward until you overcome that hurdle. For, you never hear of the person who gave up, or threw in the towel. You never remember the person who didn't finish the race or lost the prize. But the ones who are remembered, who you constantly hear about are those that persisted nonetheless, despite the obstacle and opposition. Be that person that doesn't give up, be the person that will be remembered for not backing down even though the odds were against you. Be the one who others turn to for inspiration and stay in the fight because you gave them hope.

MY DAILY WOW AFFIRMATION

I am persistent
Nothing can hold me back
I will not be discouraged
I am fierce
I am stronger

DAY 250

Everything you are going through is preparing you for what you asked for

. . .

Do not be discouraged, every challenge is helping you to build muscle to overcome the next challenge. You can and you will overcome. The person you are becoming requires the person that you are now. to grow, to be stretched, to go deeper, to push further, to climb higher. It won't be easy, but it can be done and you will be the one to do it. The person who you are becoming demands that you stand up in the midst of fear, that you let your voice be heard, that you be bold, bright and colourful. Your future self expects you to come out of the shadows, to not be ignored, to position yourself for the opportunity that will bring you in alignment with where you are supposed to be. It may not be pleasant, but it is a crucial time, it won't be long before your dreams are realised.

MY DAILY WOW AFFIRMATION

I am preparing for amazing things
I am becoming great
I am growing more like the person I want to be
I have great expectations for the future
My trials are making me better

DAY 251

Greater is in you than that which is in the world

. . .

There is a greater force working within you, than that opposing you. And that strength is constantly being renewed even in your weakness. It can be hard to rely on your own strength. At times you will need to tune into a force greater than your own. A force far bigger than you, but that operates within you and that you have access to. Even if you feel like the whole world is against you, what is fighting with you, is far more powerful than anything fighting against you. Furthermore, you have a heritage rich in culture and experience, you stand on the strength of the shoulders of all who have come before you. They made it, they survived, they withstood the opposition and that is why you are here. So do not think you stand alone against the world, rather you stand above it for you have already overcome it.

MY DAILY WOW AFFIRMATION

I am divinely protected
I have more fighting for me than against me
I will not worry
I will not be afraid
I am fearless

DAY 252

You will find a way where there seems to be none available

. . .

When something is for you, all of creation and the universe will create a path for you to follow, even if that path seems like the most challenging and difficult route to take. It will lead you to your destination. Despite countless doors that you knock on closing in your face, there will be an open door that cannot be closed because it leads you closer to your destiny, which is certain. You just have to have unshakeable faith that the path you are on, though it feels uncertain at times, is right for you. You have to have a peace within that where you are is where you are meant to be. Use your conviction as your compass to guide your decisions. And if you do not know where to go next, then life itself will present signs and direction in the form of chance and opportunities. Trust your journey.

MY DAILY WOW AFFIRMATION

I will find a way
I will find a solution to my problems
I will not be discouraged by a temporary setback
I welcome good opportunities
I am designed to succeed

DAY 253

Live without worrying

. . .

Worrying doesn't add anything to your life, in fact it robs you of your joy, kills your spirit and destroys your confidence. Stop worrying start believing. It doesn't cost you anything to have faith. And even the smallest amount of faith can make the biggest impact on your life and the lives of people around you. Live a life full of faith and belief that you will fulfil your life's purpose, this will fuel you with the energy that you need to achieve it. Worrying only depletes your energy and blocks blessings. You become closed to opportunities for fear that you will fail, or someone will let you down. Anything out of your control is not worth worrying about because it either will or won't happen. Be active about anything that is in your control, and do something about it, make the necessary change or adjustments so that you can have peace.

MY DAILY WOW AFFIRMATION

I will not worry
I will not be discouraged
I will keep going
I believe things will get better
I will achieve everything I set out to do

DAY 254

Always appreciate what you have

. . .

Everything you have is a blessing and a gift from God. Never take for granted what you have even in the midst of what you lack. You have everything you need to be all you are and all you hope to be. Be willing to share what you have in gratitude with the expectation that more will come. Be expectant that as you open up your hands to give, you are creating room to receive. Appreciate that you are loved even if it is not by the whole world, you are loved by the most important person you can be loved by and that is God. Appreciate, that you are thought dearly of, that you are in your right mind and that even the negative things in your life can turn into a positive. Be thankful that things can change and that they can turn in your favour in an instance.

MY DAILY WOW AFFIRMATION

I am grateful for all I have
I appreciate my blessings
I am thankful for my life
I know more great things will happen for me
I have positive expectations

DAY 255

Nothing worth having comes easy

. . .

Anything of great value involves great care and work to produce. It involves time and paying attention to detail. Anything worth more than what most people are willing to exchange in return for it, will involve hard work and dedication. It will not come easy and it will not happen overnight. So, the work you are putting in to be greater than you are now and the effort you are putting in to be better tomorrow than you are today is because it is worth it. And although it can be lonely and tiring getting there, the value you are obtaining far outweighs the price you are paying to get it. So, take joy in the work, because you have more enjoyment to look forward to. The easy choice may seem enjoyable for a moment, for all those that choose the easy option they soon realise that the fun is short lived.

MY DAILY WOW AFFIRMATION

I will be patient
I will work hard towards my goals
I will not get discouraged
I will persevere
I will keep progressing

DAY 256

Believe in the power you have within

. . .

When you reflect on why you doubt your abilities, at times it is because you fear that you will let yourself down and not meet your expectations. What if you make those expectations a bit more realistic? What can you do? Even if it is a menial, miniscule step or action, that seems totally insignificant. If you do this minor task several times, it will equate to something much more important. Prove to yourself that you can. Prove the lies and the doubts in your own mind to be wrong. Show yourself that even if you fail a billion times, you won't give up on yourself and you will give yourself another chance until you finally make it, get it or do it. Convince yourself that you can. Because the truth is you are capable and you can do it, so take that chance on yourself.

MY DAILY WOW AFFIRMATION

I believe in myself
I am confident in my ability
I have great skill
I am adaptable
I am evolving

DAY 257

Do it with passion or not at all

. . .

What sets you apart is your drive and energy. That is the way you make what you do unique to you. Your story and your reason for doing what you do, fuels the energy taken to get it done. What is your story? What is your reason for dreaming? What is your reason for setting goals and working towards them? Why are you working hard? Why are you planning and strategizing and working tirelessly to achieve your aspirations? Where does your energy come from? What fuels you? Your motivation gives life to your passion. Be intentional and do what you do with your motivation in sight, don't let it be a passing thought. Let it be a focus. Let it light a fire in your soul. It is the driving force to take you to where you want to go and beyond so let it serve you entirely.

MY DAILY WOW AFFIRMATION

I am passionate about my future
I am excited about my goals
I am motivated by my dreams
I am inspired by my vision
I take strategic action

DAY 258

Choose joy and peace

. . .

There are many emotions that you may feel on life's journey, some of which are harmful to you and some which will help you to get to where you want to go faster. When a situation presents itself and triggers negative emotions, take charge of your feelings, choose to be happy and appreciative in all things through joy. However, if it is a situation that is extremely difficult choose peace. You may not be able to control the situation, but you can control how you react to what has presented itself. You can reassure yourself of your strength, and inner power. You can believe that justice will prevail and that things will work in your favour. You can believe in a positive outcome even if it starts from a negative situation. And you can take the lesson rather than count the loss, take the blessing rather than count the cost.

MY DAILY WOW AFFIRMATION

I am emotionally stable
I choose happiness
I have peace
I have joy
I am not worried

DAY 259

You can rise above the storm

. . .

There is no challenge that is too big or that will overcome you. You have everything in you to succeed and to rise above any challenges that present themselves to you. Stay laser eye focused on where you are going. There is no challenge that someone has faced and not overcome. You are another example of what success looks like. You are an example of what it looks like to hope and believe that a change will come. You are what wining looks like. And although it doesn't, feel, look like or seem this way now, stay in the race. Do not give up, do not fold under the pressure, do not bow out of the fight. Hang on in there until you win. Until what you are hoping for becomes reality. Be testimony of a complete turn-around. Remember you can and you will.

MY DAILY WOW AFFIRMATION

I will rise above the storm
I will not be overwhelmed
I will not fold under pressure
I am focused
I will overcome

DAY 260

Take more risks

. . .

Often-time the greatest risks yield the biggest return. You may be averse to risks because of the fear of loss. However, losing can happen whether you take risks of not. In fact, not taking a risk is a risk within itself, because you have gambled with the chance that you may actually win and by doing nothing you have already lost. If you take the risk, you could win and even if you lose you have more chance of winning next time. Don't get complacent, laidback, or too comfortable in what seems like the easy route, take it up a gear or two, push yourself and do something that will propel you forward. Take a chance, a leap of faith, and raise your hope. It's commonly suggested that greatness is not developed in comfort zones so step out of yours and do something great!

MY DAILY WOW AFFIRMATION

I am not afraid to take risks
I am my biggest investor
I take chances on myself
I am hopeful
I operate beyond my comfort zone

DAY 261

Living a brave life comes with pain and glory

. . .

Being brave may sometimes mean standing secure in your decisions even if those decisions upset some people. And that is ok because there are a few brave things you may need to do to allow you to rise and fulfil purpose. Being brave may mean that you stand up in adversity, or that you speak up against injustice. However, you cannot afford not to be brave because your very being requires it from you in order for you to be all that you can be. Liberty is attached to your bravery; your own liberty and the liberty of lives you may not even know you have an impact on. Although being brave is a choice, you always have to decide to be brave as the consequence of not being brave can be detrimental to you and to those attached to you. Don't worry you will never regret being brave

MY DAILY WOW AFFIRMATION

I am brave
I do not fear
I stand in faith
I am bold
I am liberated

288

DAY 262

Never ever give up

. . .

Everyone at some point in their life feels like their pursuit of achievement, in a particular area is a waste of effort and therefore they consider quitting. However, the difference between the successful and the ones that are not, is that, for the successful, it is just a consideration. They thoughtfully weigh out the options and are able to convince themselves that their efforts are for a worthy cause, and the worth of success in that endeavour is of more value than the effort it takes to get there. Be that person that takes careful consideration and concludes it is a worthy cause, not just for success but because of the person you become after making that decision. A person of integrity, determination, unwavering, victorious, consistent, reliable. There is no way you won't continue to succeed if you choose not to give up at every experience of conflict or adversity.

MY DAILY WOW AFFIRMATION

I will not give up
I will not stop
I will not be defeated
I am a conqueror
I am victorious

DAY 263

Be you

. . .

The beauty of creativity is that it is an expression of uniqueness. You were created and engineered with exclusivity. There is no one existing or who has ever existed that is you. That makes you considerably precious and valuable. There is a need for you and what you bring, your voice, your perception, your ideology, your movement and physicality is essential. You are important, you are special, you are necessary. But if you are mimicking someone else how can we access the beauty of your individuality? How can we understand your exceptional worth? It is crucial that you remain you, that you do not lose yourself in this world by turning into everyone else. The world needs you to remain you, even if you grow and develop or transform. Transform into a better version of yourself and not anyone else. Because you are the creator's gift to the world.

MY DAILY WOW AFFIRMATION

I am unique
I am creative
I have a special gift
I am relevant
I am important

DAY 264

Dream it and then do it

. . .

Do whatever you can do to make that dream a reality. Whether it is a vision of yourself achieving something remarkable or a vision of a unique experience, product or service. Do whatever it takes to make it happen. This dream was given to you as a gift because you have something in you to see it through. Start working towards fulfilling this vison. Share it with someone you trust that has a desire to see you flourish and succeed. Search for guidance on how you can build on the knowledge you have. Search for opportunities that will put you in a better position for your dream to be a success. Do whatever it takes because the fulfilment of that dream depends on more than your success but will benefit the lives of many. Put the work in and you will see the results that will make your dream a reality.

MY DAILY WOW AFFIRMATION

I will accomplish my goals
I will fulfil my destiny
I will complete my journey
I will realise my dreams
I will succeed

DAY 265

Remember who you are

. . .

You are distinct, powerful and necessary. You were created by the highest form of intelligence. There's nothing about you that is a mistake. You are the answer to unanswered questions. You are the solution to unsolved problems. Your unique perception, ideology and expression is essential. And it doesn't matter who doesn't understand it or know it. You have to recognise and know it first. You must own who you are in order for the standard to be raised. Silence the voices and tune into yourself, your strongest most powerful and confident self, that exists but may have been lying dormant because of all the external prisons. The time is now and you are free to be who you were created to be, despite what is happening around you. It is time for you to stand strong in your divine purpose, which is for you but much bigger than you.

MY DAILY WOW AFFIRMATION

I am in control of my destiny
I know who I am
I know what I want
I am unassuming
I am making decisions that serve my purpose

DAY 266

Once you become fearless, life becomes limitless

. . .

Fear is a liar. It is not real. Being careful or cautious is not fear it is wisdom. You do not fear getting burnt you know you will get burnt if you come in contact with fire, that is a fact. But being anxious about things that are not factual, is a choice, it is a response to uncertainty or reaction to lack of control. This choice restricts you and can even imprison you. Do not let this happen. Rather use it as an opportunity to live a life of faith, choose to feel hopeful for the best results, despite not knowing the outcome. Choose to believe that you will find favour and blessings and that one way or another things will work out. This way you position yourself for countless opportunities, rather than settling for the one bad result.

MY DAILY WOW AFFIRMATION

I will not fear
I am limitless
I will not be held back
I will press forward
I will always find favour

DAY 267

The decision you make in this very moment affects the course of your life

. . .

Make your decisions wisely for they form the path to your destination. Don't be blasé in what you choose to do in the moment. Don't be passive with an authority that has been given to you, that impacts you and those around you. Be intentional with your decision making. Consider the benefits to yourself first and then to those immediately around you. How much do you want to be the person you have the full potential of becoming? How much is it worth to you to put in the disciplines that will shape your character tomorrow? Character cannot be bought, it is earned through self-control, discipline and consistency. What you are trying to achieve is incredibly worth it however you have to be willing to sacrifice temporary pleasure for long-term enjoyment. And you are capable of doing just that. The more you do not give in the easier it becomes to overcome temptations.

MY DAILY WOW AFFIRMATION

I control the course of my life
I will make wise decisions
I act in faith
I am refining my character
My steps are intentional

DAY 268

Your only limit is you, be brave and fearless

. . .

You are limitless, you really have no idea what you cannot do until you attempt to do it, you may fail several times then eventually succeed and even surprise yourself. Perhaps something you once thought was impossible is now easy. Don't walk in fear and miss out on a fantastic opportunity to be great. Be brave and confront your fear by acting despite the concerns you have of the outcome. And then keep trying until you are able to convince yourself that you are in control of the outcome and possess the power to create an outcome that favours you. Start to think up results that you desire and work tirelessly to make them happen. You have everything you need in you to become the success that you visualise, you just have to take that first leap of faith and then keep leaping until you reach your goal.

MY DAILY WOW AFFIRMATION

I am brave

I am fearless

I am not limited

I will reach my goals

I will be successful

DAY 269

Don't be afraid of failure for it is the bridge you need to get across to the other side

. . .

It is often said of successful people that they failed their way to success. On a journey even if you have a map, you may miss your way, or the road may be blocked. It doesn't mean you should stop. You simply must find another route. You must make another attempt but this time with the knowledge you have gained from your setback, fall, or loss. You will never know whether you will be a success or not if you continue to give up at every challenge you face. You must continue to try, despite the obstacle. There are countless testimonials of people overcoming in the face of adversity in what seems like opposition that was impossible to beat. But they won. So what hinders you? Is the excuse so great it robs you of your chance to break through? No, you are far more stronger and resilient than anything that is against you.

MY DAILY WOW AFFIRMATION

I will use my failures as lessons
I will not be discouraged if I fall
I will learn from my mistakes
I will use my lesson as a bridge to my success
I will use what I have learned to overcome

DAY 270

Be unwavering in the pursuit of purpose

. . .

Have the outright audacity to believe that your desire to achieve and live out your purpose is valid. It is so valid that you don't mind knocking on a thousand doors if you have to, with the knowledge that one of those doors will make everything fall into place like it should. Your belief in your passions being realised are so valid that you don't mind stepping out of your comfort zone and pushing the boundaries to get to where you need to go and be in rooms where vital decisions are being made, that can alter the course of your life. Choose to live a bold, confident life to pursue your passion and achieve your desires. What you are trying to pursue may sound ludicrous to those around you but it is with your tenacity and daring ability to believe, that will be the driving force for what you require to manifest.

MY DAILY WOW AFFIRMATION

I am passionate about my purpose
I will pursue my vision
I will make well thought through decisions
I will be bold
I am confident that I will make it

DAY 271

Have no regrets about being brave

. . .

Take that leap of faith, even if you fail, you learn, you grow, you get stronger, tougher, more resilient. Never miss a chance to be better and do better. You will never regret standing up to fear and feeling the power of being invincible. You will never regret feeling strong and believing in yourself. Because these are the very tools you need to make it to where you want to go. There will be times when you have to stand alone. There will be times when you have to fight giants. There will be times when you have to speak up and let your voice be heard. Despite the outcome in that moment you are the victor, the hero the champion who faced their fears for a greater cause. Keep that in mind because there will be many times when you will need to use that bravery again.

MY DAILY WOW AFFIRMATION

I will be brave
I will trust my journey
I will yield to my process
I will own my strength
I will tap into my inner power

DAY 272

Pain is momentary, greatness is forever

. . .

Adversity, discomfort, challenges are all time bound, they do not last forever. In fact, they usually are short-lived especially when you have the audacity to visualise how great things look when the negatives come to an end. Once you can see a better picture; you can hope. And hope changes things. Hope creates opportunities that seemed not to have existed before. Those opportunities exercised turn into a series of triumphs and successes. And what seemed to be painful and suffering turns into greatness and achievement. Do not miss out on the opportunity to be great because of temporary obstacles. Those obstacles can be overcome, and you can be the one to overcome them through your ability to see what you can gain by looking beyond the difficulty that presents itself now. You are bigger, better, stronger and more intelligent than what your situation looks like now.

MY DAILY WOW AFFIRMATION

The pain I feel is temporary
The character I am building is long-lasting
What I am going through is worth it
I am hopeful
I welcome great opportunities

DAY 273

Believe in the person you are becoming

. . .

If you are going to take a chance on anybody, take a chance on yourself. You owe it to yourself and you are worthy enough to make that huge investment. Believing in something that hasn't occurred is a big risk. But if you are going to take any risks, let it be one that you have some say or control over the stakes. Take a chance on yourself. For you know what it is that you have to do to get to where you want to be. You just have to be willing. And that willingness is tied to your self-worth. Are you worth the sacrifice it will take to become who you know you should be? Of course you are. But you have to believe it and live that truth daily. You have to understand this temporary sacrifice and risk is worth everything you are doing.

MY DAILY WOW AFFIRMATION

I believe in the person I am becoming
I am investing in me
The sacrifices I am making are worth it
My worth is immeasurable
I believe I am precious

DAY 274

Your strength is greater than you think it is

. . .

You do not know your full strength until you face a situation when you need to exercise it. And more often than not many people underestimate their true strength; for they cannot foresee how they would cope if they faced adversity or came across a particular challenge. However, what many do not realise is that their very make up and design is to handle adversity from conception to death. Exercising your strength is completely correlated to your growth. You are constantly growing, that may not be something that you are aware of because it happens naturally and without your control, simply put, that is life. And an inherent part of life is survival, which is overcoming adversity. To overcome adversity is your ability to use the power within. These powers are innate, they are part of who you are and are there to serve you. So, stop discounting yourself and use them.

MY DAILY WOW AFFIRMATION

I am strong

I am powerful

There is no challenge I cannot overcome

I can rise above adversity

I will not underestimate my ability

DAY 275

The most precious things happen unexpectedly

. . .

There are some things that you cannot predict, or control. You just have to wait for it. Wait and trust that when everything that needs to happen has happened, what you desire will come to pass. If it hasn't happened yet do everything you need to do to prepare for it, so that it will be long-lasting and not temporary. Focus your energy on other areas in your life that need work. Keep progressing and becoming a better version of yourself. When you are ready and possibly when you are not expecting it, what you desire will be made available to you. When it arrives, you will be prepared and know what to do so that it will be sustainable and it will not be short-lived. Something great does not occur overnight but takes time and detailed investment. Be patient and wait for it. It will surely come, just get ready.

MY DAILY WOW AFFIRMATION

I believe everything will work out
I believe in due time what is for me will come to me
I am confident that my time is coming
Good things are coming my way
Great things are happening in my life

DAY 276

Live without fear of the future

. . .

Stop worrying about things that exist only in your imagination. God will not and has not given up on you. Think on things that are true, pure and factual. Have hope in the future that things will improve, that the results will be for your growth, elevation and favour. Even if for a short while it seems difficult, rest in the fact that this discomfort will not last forever. Better is coming, the morning of a new day will come and the dark clouds will disappear. Stop living in regret and replaying mistakes, that are in the past, you have control to determine your future. What will you choose? Or will you let external factors determine your fate? Be intentional and active about what you want for the future. You are deserving of so much more, even if you feel unworthy. It is through humility that you rise and grow.

MY DAILY WOW AFFIRMATION

Everything will work itself out
I am being divinely guided
My steps are secure
I am unshakeable
I will get to my destination

DAY 277

What you do now determines where you will be mentally, physically and financially

. . .

What you do today in this moment will determine your tomorrow and the subsequent days after that. It is vital that your choices serve your best interest and help you to develop either mentally, spiritually or financially. These are areas of your life that are crucial for you to have a fulfilling and meaningful existence. To assist in making the best decisions that keep you on course to achieve desired results, you need a good support system. This can be people that are already present in your life or mentors that you follow closely. Some of your choices may require you to take the necessary steps of faith to put you in a completely different place from where you are now. Take that leap and enjoy the benefits of walking by faith, not seeking the approval of others but being secure in your new found self-awareness.

MY DAILY WOW AFFIRMATION

I am making decisions that serve my purpose
I am improving financially
I am growing spiritually
I am developing emotionally
I am becoming mentally stronger

DAY 278

Remind yourself of all the battles you have won, and all the fears you have overcome

. . .

When facing an obstacle that you are finding challenging to overcome you have to remind yourself of past victories. What have you faced that was initially difficult, that you got through? At the time you may have been anxious, you may have felt like when is this all going to end. You may have felt like a failure, or had to recover from some sort of defeat. But whatever you faced, you made it through, you are alive to tell the tale. What did you do? How did you make it through? What did you do to overcome? What mind-set did you adopt? What did you learn? Now use those same principles to tackle this battle even if it's a completely different scenario, you can still use the winning mind set or lessons learned to combat this current challenge. You have won before, you can win again.

MY DAILY WOW AFFIRMATION

I am successful

I am a winner

I am an overcomer

I will not be stopped by fear

I am a conqueror

DAY 279

You haven't been buried; you have been planted

. . .

When you are in complete darkness and feel like you have been isolated, forgotten and submerged. Do not fret. This is an opportunity for you to take record of who you have been in the past. The comfort and protection that once surrounded you is no longer there, you have been left to depend on no one but yourself. Therefore, embrace your new surroundings, even though it feels unfamiliar, let go of any inhibition. You were placed here to grow. So, soak in every lesson and anything that can fuel you, use it to rise. And once you start rising you will eventually rise out of that darkness to encounter light. That light will further help you to grow and your true beauty will be revealed. In growing you will produce fruit, which will yield seed, generating a legacy, just because you chose to follow-through with your process.

MY DAILY WOW AFFIRMATION

I am being nurtured
I am growing
I am developing
I will be fruitful
I will expand my reach

DAY 280

Rest, recovery and reflection are just as essential as the grind if you want to be successful

. . .

Working hard is very important, working intelligently is even more important, consistently working is crucial, because you need something to build from and towards. However, you cannot consistently work if you do not schedule in time to rest, you will burn out. Your strength needs to be renewed. You need a time to recover and refuel. You need time to reflect on whether the work you are doing is actually effective or whether you need to make slight changes to what it is that you are doing in order to accomplish what it is that you want to achieve. Resting is just as important as working, grinding, hustling or putting in the hours, especially if you want what you build to last. Rest is more than sleeping, it is shutting yourself away from what consumes your energy. Hence why rest has to be accompanied by refuelling so you do not get burnt out.

MY DAILY WOW AFFIRMATION

I am being renewed
I balance my activity with rest
Operating at my best is important to me
I conserve my energy
I will remain consistent

DAY 281

If you do not ask,
the answer will be no

. . .

A lot of the answers to the questions you have, are on the other side of you asking the right questions to the right people at the right time. Such as, do you know where I can get...? Can you help with...? Can you give me...? The challenge may be you do not know when, who and what to ask. Then just start with asking. If they do not have the answer you want, they may know or may lead you to the person who does. Keep asking until you get the answer. The answer will always be no, if you do not ask, so search for your yes. That yes will turn everything around and put you in a position to receive more yesses and those yesses will open doors and put you in positions where you can start saying yes and providing answers to someone's unanswered questions.

MY DAILY WOW AFFIRMATION

I will be bold
I will go for what I want from life
I will not be afraid to ask for help when I need it
I will pursue my desires
I will be active in my pursuits

DAY 282

Do not strive for perfection, be the best version of yourself that you can be

. . .

Be your best and most authentic self, it not only liberates you, but those around you. Perfection is a myth, it doesn't really exist. It is something to aspire to but is very rarely achieved. The reason for this is we are constantly evolving and improving, so our definition of perfection will change. Therefore, can anyone really be perfect? If perfect is only perfect but for a while? If the answer is no, then, aim to be the best, there is no limit on what the best is, the best is always improving, developing and growing. Someone can meet you at perfection, no one can meet you at being the best. And if your competition is yourself then outdo yourself, come back harder and stronger. When your competition is yourself you are untouchable, as you are not limited by the people around you, you are on a whole dimension of your own, on another level entirely.

MY DAILY WOW AFFIRMATION

I am a work in progress
I am a masterpiece
I strive for excellence
I strive to be and do my best
I am working hard to become better

DAY 283

Be unstoppable
you deserve better

. . .

Keep going and don't stop until you get everything your heart desires. You are worth all the hard work, sleepless nights, sweat, blood and tears. All the dedication you have put in should be rewarded with the highest accolades. When you are going for the top, sadly people think they have the right to tell you how far you should go, like their opinion actually matters. Respectfully ignore them and keep going. You determine how far you want to go. You know your significance, value, and the investment you have made. Do not let anyone hinder or discourage you for wanting more. Do not let them define you by their own limitations. Do what is needed for you and where you need to be. Do not settle, do not give in, do not discount or discredit yourself, you are deserving of everything you are going for and more.

MY DAILY WOW AFFIRMATION

I am unstoppable
I deserve the best
I am going for better
My opinions are valid
I am a valuable investment

DAY 284

Your outlook influences your outcome and your attitude determines your altitude

. . .

What you see will impact how you act. Your view, perception and vision will greatly affect the decisions you make. There are so many ways to look at things and then to transform this into a form of thought process to gain understanding of what you see. Your thought process is a choice. Anyone can look at something but how you choose to understand what you see and allow this to have a bearing on your decision is a choice you make. Likewise, the manner in which you choose to act is a choice. The power of that choice lies with you. The result is directly linked to your decision based on your thought process. Therefore, cultivate a positive outlook for a positive outcome, adopt a great attitude for a great altitude. You can only get out what you put in. If you want greatness, see with the eyes of greatness.

MY DAILY WOW AFFIRMATION

I will adopt a positive attitude
I determine my direction in life
I will have a better outlook on life
I will expect great outcomes
I anticipate good things to happen

DAY 285

Use what you've been through as fuel to get to where you want to go

. . .

You didn't go through everything you've been through to just remain in the same place and be the same person that you have always been. Your experiences are there to shape you and help you to grow. Both good and bad experiences are there for you to learn and become a better version of yourself. Use them as fuel to propel you forward. It's not good enough to have the knowledge, experience gives you the muscle you need to adopt the stance required for the next position you need to be in. It is time to use what you have been through to jump higher, run further and fly faster. Do not be ashamed of your past mistakes or be discouraged over injustice, share your story and grow. Use it as fuel to propel you forward for better and greater things, which you are so deserving of.

MY DAILY WOW AFFIRMATION

My experiences have made me wiser
I am better because I have learnt from previous failures
I am knowledgeable
I have more understanding
I am flourishing

DAY 286

Look after yourself, self-care is vital for your development

. . .

Your body innately renews itself and looks after itself by fighting off disease and illness, also it signals to you when you need food or rest. It does this so that you can grow and be your strongest self. The worst thing you can do for your body is ignore it when it is communicating to you to do the very thing that will benefit your growth. Do whatever it takes to take care of yourself. Protect yourself by creating boundaries from people that do not support your elevation. Feed your body, mind, spirit and soul with food that will nourish you deeply and give you strength to continue on your journey. Take time out to plug out, shut everything off and completely and utterly rest, so you have the chance to regenerate energy for all the upcoming tasks. You need you to survive, be strong, healthy and happy.

MY DAILY WOW AFFIRMATION

I make self-care a priority
My health is important to me
I protect my energy
I do not let anyone cross my boundaries
I rest when I need to

DAY 287

What defines us is how well we rise after falling

. . .

Your failures do not define you, it is what you choose to do after you fail. Do you fall and wallow in self-pity or learn and rise? Falling is not the problem it is choosing not to rise each time you fall, that will hinder you. It is not how many times or how hard you fall that is important it is how quick and how high you rise. Do not stay down, do not remain defeated. Keep rising and striving to stand, hold onto your posture. And even if you fall, try again, acknowledging why you fell and promise yourself you will not fall like that another time and even if you do you will rise and you will keep on rising until you are too high for anyone or anything to bring you down. It is harder to fall when you have built a strong foundation and risen with humility and integrity.

MY DAILY WOW AFFIRMATION

I will continue to rise
I will not be defeated
I will always find a way to get up when I fall
I will not be discouraged by a setback
I will not give up

DAY 288

Changing who you are to be accepted will leave you feeling disappointed

. . .

Always remain true and be the authentic version of yourself. Don't dilute the essence of who you are to fit into the status quo, you are only enhancing the void you are trying to fill. Attaching your happiness to the praise of people and placing them in control of your emotions is very dangerous. The benchmark always changes, so while you are doing all you can to find validation, you will continue without ever being satisfied. Be you, like what you like and do what you do. Someone that embraces their imperfection but strives for the best is always respected and admired. Validating yourself gives you inner peace and confidence that will liberate you on every dimension. You are whole and complete and need not be endorsed by anyone other than yourself. Seeking external approval will always leave you empty and unfulfilled.

MY DAILY WOW AFFIRMATION

I will not change who I am to be externally validated
I validate myself
I have self-confidence
I am at peace with myself
I love who I am and who I am becoming

DAY 289

It is when you feel like quitting that the breakthrough is closest

. . .

Think about all the work you have put in. Everything you have sacrificed and although it seems like you have worked so hard and it hasn't given you the results you want yet., this is not the time to give up or throw in the towel. In fact, more now than ever before you have to push through your feelings and press on. You are closest to the prize than you have ever been. Your victory will soon await you and it is on the other side of this last hurdle you have to jump over. Don't forfeit all the blessings that could be yours if only you remain in the fight. Don't forfeit all the effort you've put in and let it go to waste because you feel discouraged. To think of starting again is far more difficult than continuing where you are. Rest, re-energise but do not under any circumstance give up.

MY DAILY WOW AFFIRMATION

My breakthrough is near
I will not quit
I will not fold under pressure
I will push through
I will advance

DAY 290

Focus on your strengths

. . .

Mastering one thing at a time is key. Focus on what you are good at, what comes naturally to you or what you can do without putting in much effort. Refine this and let it add value to your life. Then address areas of your life that require further improvement, areas that will build your character and give you a good reputation. Once you have mastered this and you are confident in your strengths as well as your ability to improve, study your weaknesses, be a student of areas in your life where you feel like a failure. Work on what you can do to be better, then make better good and good great. From here the hardest challenge will be to create balance and maintain the excellence you have established. But the foundation is being secure in your strength and knowing what that is.

MY DAILY WOW AFFIRMATION

I am refining my strengths
I am improving in areas where I am weak
I am becoming my best self
I am working on being better
I will remain focused

DAY 291

Believe you can do it, believe you deserve it and believe you will get it

. . .

Your ability is not the issue it is your belief system. Do you really believe you can? Whether you deserve it or not is irrelevant it is whether you believe you deserve it. The answer to this is in your self-evaluation and who validates you. Do you validate yourself or do you wait for other people to validate you? Are you living up to the expectations of other people or in the knowledge you have of yourself and all you know you should be? You are exactly who you are determined to be. If you are determined to become something you will find a way, you will turn that can't into can and that won't into will. You are more than deserving of every blessing that comes your way not because of who you are, but who you will become and use that position to bless. Believe in yourself, believing changes everything.

MY DAILY WOW AFFIRMATION

I believe I can do it
I believe I am deserving of every blessing in my life
I believe I will get everything I am working for
I will achieve my goals
I will get to my destination

DAY 292

Be unstoppable despite your failures, doubts or how many times you fall

. . .

Don't let anything stop you from pursuing your goals, aspirations or vision. No matter how many times you fall or fail, pick yourself up, dust yourself off and keep going. Doubts may creep up and fill your head unexpectedly, these come to cloud your vision. Do not let it override what you know is true, and that is you are more than capable of achieving wonderful things if you do not give up. Keep shining the light on your dreams by declaring your positive affirmations daily. Do not be overcome by the struggle or challenge, press and push through. Fight through the barriers, kick down every wall, jump over every hurdle for you are more than a conqueror and you have a force fighting for you that is stronger than you are. They can't break you or stop you, so keep on going and be the winner you already are.

MY DAILY WOW AFFIRMATION

I am unstoppable
I will not be defeated
I will not be discouraged
I will not be held back by fear
I will not be hindered by doubt

DAY 293

Your passion is a powerful force to propel you towards your destiny

. . .

You may question what your purpose is and feel lost because you do not have a clear answer to give which relates to a single vocation pertaining to something significant in your life. Your purpose is linked to your passion. And that does not have to be a singular entity, it can be several things that stir you up and get you excited about life. A worthy cause to fight for, an ideology that brings a solution to a problem yet to be solved; It could be an expression of creativity that provides a platform for others to relate to and identify with; It could be bringing people together for a common cause despite differences of background, ethnicity or creed. Whatever your passion is, nurture it, study it, develop it and invest in it. It will guide you to a place that is bigger than you could ever imagine.

MY DAILY WOW AFFIRMATION

I am powerful
I am authentic
I am passionate about my destiny
My purpose propels me forward
I am advancing daily

DAY 294

Invest your energy in the things that will add value to your life and the lives of others

. . .

Your energy once directed effectively can serve you greatly. It can propel you closer to your goals and visions. Often people and situations will seek to use your energy for purposes outside of what benefits you. Do not allow this. Rather consider only using your energy for things that add value to your life. Protect your energy at all cost by creating boundaries. It is not everyone in your life that is worthy of your time, it is not every situation that occurs that is worthy of your attention. Understand which things in your life require your energy because it leads to your elevation. Position yourself so that you can be poured into when you are running on empty. It is so crucial that the people around you and the spaces you dwell in are conducive for your growth. To avoid delays and being taken off course make sure you are investing your energy wisely.

MY DAILY WOW AFFIRMATION

My energy is precious
I invest my energy appropriately
I add value wherever I go
I am committed to growth
I use my time effectively

DAY 295

Bravery is continuing in the midst of fear and is not the absence of fear

. . .

Being brave doesn't mean you are not anxious about the outcome; it is continuing despite being fearful. And you must be brave in order to be successful. You have to be brave enough to say no when yes does not serve you. You have to be brave enough to leave when staying delays you. You have to be brave to stand up and stand alone when sitting discredits your integrity. You must be brave despite the fear of rejection, loneliness and oppression. Being brave is not glamourous it can actually be absolutely terrifying. But the rewards far outweigh the initial discomfort. The victory makes being brave sweet and worth every negative thought entertained temporarily. Because the outcome of being brave usually is winning. The outcome of being brave is becoming stronger and letting your opposition know you won't take defeat. So, do all you can to be brave and be bold.

MY DAILY WOW AFFIRMATION

I am brave
I do not let fear stop me
I will not give up
I will pursue my dreams
I will achieve everything I set my heart upon

DAY 296

Love yourself more

. . .

You cannot pour from an empty cup, and if you pour from a cup half full it will also soon have nothing left. Therefore, love from a place of fullness. Where you are so full, it overflows to those around you naturally. Love from a place where it is not a burden, where you can freely give and receive with no expectation, because you are content. Be kind to yourself, patient with yourself and honest with yourself. Understand what is good and bad for you. And do more of what is good for you, avoiding the things that are bad for you. Love yourself without condition, despite your imperfections. You are worthy of love and when you know how to love yourself, you are better at receiving it, recognising it is a gift that you are worthy of. Give yourself the best gift you can and that is love.

MY DAILY WOW AFFIRMATION

I am devoted to doing what is best for my well-being
I am committed to self-care
I love who I am and who I am becoming
I am striving to be my best
It is important to me to do what is right for me

DAY 297

Everything will happen at the appropriate time

. . .

The good, the bad and the ugly all have their place and serve their purpose. Everything you have been through, even the mistakes that you feel you have made, all serve their purpose. The misfortune, the wrongdoings, the injustices, although while it lasts it feels unbearable, it all serves its purpose. For how can we have light without darkness and what would day be without night? Sun without rain and hot without cold? We shun and hate wickedness and yes good must triumph over evil, but even if it feels like life is nothing but negative, it is but for a while. It is temporary and will pass. While you wait, pray and hope, allow peace to fill your heart with the knowledge that in the end, you win and all will be well. No matter how low you go be encouraged, it will work out to favour you.

MY DAILY WOW AFFIRMATION

Everything will work out in my favour
Everything I need will come into my life at the right time
Great things are happening for me
Every negativity will be removed from my life
I trust the timing of my life

DAY 298

Painful situations can teach us lessons that we didn't ever think we needed to know

. . .

A painful situation is not designed because you needed to learn from it. Learning from it is a choice that you have to consciously make. Especially if that pain came from vulnerability, where the people that were supposed to protect you, did not and you were left to devices beyond your control, broken and torn. It is not because you deserved it or because you did anything wrong. And whether you understand the situation or not, looking at it retrospectively, does not change the fact that your experience was not what you would have chosen for yourself. However, it happened, and you have to choose how it's impact will steer the course of your life during your process of healing and recovery. There is now something you know about life more than anyone else, because you have lived it and overcome it and perhaps are still overcoming it.

MY DAILY WOW AFFIRMATION

I will gain from my pain
I will learn from my struggle
My suffering is temporary
I will not give up
I will not stop fighting

DAY 299

Do what you love with passion or not at all

. . .

When you have a skill that is also your most favourite thing to do in the world, do it with every fibre of your being, every time and all the time. Deliver it with grace. Use it to tell your story, be soft and vulnerable with it, allow it to display your courage and strength. Do not be lazy, passive or blasé with it. This is your gift to the world, for you to enjoy but also for you to help others to heal, become liberated and, encouraged. This gift is bigger than you, so do not take it for granted. Nurture it and refine it, grow it and develop it, then share it, make it available and accessible. Study, perfect and master it. Use it to teach people and enlighten them. If you abuse your gift, it may be taken away, so protect it, cherish it, and love it with passion.

MY DAILY WOW AFFIRMATION

I am passionate about my future
I love the person I am becoming
I am empowered by my purpose
I am excited by my future
I will execute on my plans

DAY 300

The question is not can you? The question is, will you?

. . .

Whether you have the ability or not is irrelevant especially when you haven't even tried. However, are you willing to do whatever it takes for however long it takes until it is done. Working hard can pay off, but working with intelligence will pay with dividends. This is simply because when you apply intelligence you make it work by finding a way. With intelligence you know the outcome, you are just determining which is the most effective way to reach that outcome. Some questions are really just doubt or fear exposing themselves. The answer is based on your confidence and desire. Do you really want it or do you have an excuse? The answer will always be it is possible, it is just up to you to prove how it is possible by applying your intelligence with relentlessness to make it happen.

MY DAILY WOW AFFIRMATION

I will accomplish my goals
I will achieve greatness
I will work hard to execute my vision
I will not stop until I get to my destination
I will continue until I am successful

DAY 301

Don't entertain the thought of giving up

. . .

So many miss out on great opportunities and vast fortunes because right at the tip of a breakthrough they feel like they just can't hold on any longer and they decide to quit. Do not let that be you. You haven't come this far and worked this hard to forsake the crown rewarded for your efforts. You must press on. Rest if you need to, but do not quit. Giving up isn't even an option, there is too much at stake. The very essence of who you are trying to become is riding on you seeing it through to the end. You have to persevere. Do whatever it takes. Seek help if you need to, to make it across the finish line. Keep your eye on the prize, the great and glorious prize of making it despite the many challenges. Everything in you is engineered for success. Do what you were born to do; win.

MY DAILY WOW AFFIRMATION

I am not a quitter
I will complete my journey
I will complete the task at hand
I will not forsake my reward
I will hold on until the end

DAY 302

You are mighty and fierce enough to overcome your fears

. . .

You have a fighting spirit inside of you. A spirit that will not bow down to oppression or victimisation. A fighting spirit that will overthrow injustice and silence terror. Fear is an oppressor; it imprisons its victims unfairly and terrorises them by heightening their weaknesses. Awaken the fighter in you and overcome fear, destroy it and eradicate it from your life. Shut it down and annihilate it as it serves no purpose for where you are going. You are stronger and much more wiser than fear. Your weapons are more powerful and effective and you stand with a power greater than you, that will support you all the way; through friends, family and other overcomers. Fear is weak, it is a tiny voice that parades itself as a giant, it is a trickster, but you are armed with the truth, you can and you will defeat it entirely.

MY DAILY WOW AFFIRMATION

I am fierce
I will overcome my fears
I will not let fear intimidate me
What I carry in me is greater than any obstacle
Greatness is on the other side of fear

DAY 303

Be you at your best

. . .

There is only one of you, so make sure you are the best you, that you can possibly be. There is no competition except for the competition to be better than you were yesterday. Your industry may be saturated, but there is only one you. That already sets you apart from the rest, now enhance that authenticity with the spirit of excellence. Be more of all you can be. Give more of all you can give, do more of all you can do. This is operating at your best. This is being in a league of your own with no comparison or competition. This is you operating at your optimum and maximum potential. You are capable of great things so expand on that and start delivering greatness every time. Ask yourself is this good or great and always make sure it is great when it is completed.

MY DAILY WOW AFFIRMATION

I am authentic
I am unique
I will commit to giving my best
I will endeavour to do my best
I will operate with a spirit of excellence

DAY 304

Let no one discourage your ambitions

. . .

At times life will require you to be your own coach, cheerleader, fan, and still play on the field. Leave the commentators to watch from the side lines, you are too focused on the prize for their opinions to be relevant. You said you would win and that is exactly what you are going to do. Score, cheer and celebrate. Give them a show while they watch, let them watch in amazement and continue to question how you do it. While they are wondering, keep practicing, perfecting and mastering your craft. Keep working on yourself, so that when it is time to perform, you show up and show out. You are the star player in your own game, you are counting on you, to bring the trophy home. They may doubt your ability, but prove the doubters wrong you have everything it takes and more to get exactly what you are going for.

MY DAILY WOW AFFIRMATION

I will be kind to myself
I will encourage myself
I will celebrate wins
I will commit to practicing
I will focus on winning

DAY 305

Stay strong

. . .

Anything you are working hard to accomplish and believing will come to pass, needs you to remain dedicated. Don't lose hope, stay in the fight and stand strong. Stay focused, do not get distracted or complacent. Do not get comfortable and fall into a trap of false security. Do not be tempted to become too relaxed about your goals, dreams and ambitions, they will not materialise themselves, they need to be worked on and you need to build towards them. You have started well but you must continue, and continue wholeheartedly, give it all you have without holding back. Resist the urge to rest prematurely. Rest when you need to not when you feel like it. Exercise discipline as this will build your mental stamina to endure for long. You have already demonstrated your strength just keep being who you already are as you can and will make it.

MY DAILY WOW AFFIRMATION

I will not allow discouragement to overcome me
I will not be tempted to quit
I will stand strong
I will hold on
I will keep fighting

DAY 306

Embrace the journey

. . .

The road can get rough and rocky sometimes but keep at it. You are on the right path. Don't try and bail out or take the simpler route. The road to anything worthwhile is always less appealing to travel on, but this rough and difficult road is the most rewarding. Embrace the journey. For it will produce in you everything you need for the person you are working on becoming. You will make it to your destination, you will successfully climb every mountain, get through every valley and cross every river. There is no challenge on this journey that will stop you. Do not be so fixated with a specific route, as it is the destination that matters and there are many routes to one destination. Live and enjoy whichever route you choose to take. For it will teach you and develop you for even greater success.

MY DAILY WOW AFFIRMATION

I will embrace my journey
I will enjoy the process
I will see my journey through to the end
I will learn, develop and grow
I will reach my destination

DAY 307

Your past mistakes are meant to guide you, not define you

. . .

Don't get stuck in the past or weighed down by mistakes. Rather, use it as ammunition, a force to push you to where you want to go. Don't be discouraged because you tried and failed, you are not a failure, you are a student and every time you get it wrong, you are closer to getting it right. Every time you make a mistake, it is not to expose your weaknesses, but to address them and turn them into strengths. Each time you go off course, it is to show you which way not to take and to guide you back on track. Do not get stuck in a place which was only meant to teach you., Be a student; get the experience, learn and move on. That lesson does not define who you are, because you are constantly evolving and becoming wiser through the knowledge and understanding you gain.

MY DAILY WOW AFFIRMATION

I will not be defined by my past mistakes
I am not a failure
I am a student of life
I am stronger than I think
I am greater than who I was yesterday

DAY 308

Do more than just exist

. . .

Your existence is important but make it significant also. There are many people that travel the earth, some further than others, but there are few that make a long-lasting impact. The sort of impact that lasts for generations to come. You become significant by living a full, fulfilled life. There is a gift inside of you that is unique to you, its engineered into your DNA and is for you to enjoy, use and share this gift with as many people as you can. Identifying this gift is key, it is what you do naturally without a thought, it is what you are passionate about and could do without request or a fee. Whatever you do make sure you are using your gift because it is not only for you, but it is for every soul that will be reached by it, now and for generations to come.

MY DAILY WOW AFFIRMATION

I am determined to live my best life
I am living a life of purpose
My life has meaning
I will use my gift to bless the world
I am engineered with greatness

DAY 309

Sometimes it takes being completely lost to be found

. . .

It is ok to not know it all. Anyone at any time can get lost, it happens sometimes. You may find yourself completely stuck or off course with no idea of how to get back on track. This is a time to reflect and be honest with yourself. Where did you lose your way? At which point did you take the wrong turn? Did you ever really know where you were going? What do you need to do to get back on track? Who do you need to reach out to or ask for help from? It's humbling and it will take you out of your comfort zone. But this vulnerability makes you human and relatable. Most people at some point in their life have been lost so they are happy to help guide you to where you need to go. Let them find and help you.

MY DAILY WOW AFFIRMATION

I promise to always be honest with myself
I was lost now I am found
I am getting back on track
I will not let distractions stop me
I will push through every barrier

DAY 310

Do not be motivated by fear

. . .

Fear robs you of the joy that comes with achieving and reaching your goals. Fear of loss, fear of lack, fear of rejection. These are negative motivators and although they may get you to where you want to be, you rarely enjoy the journey or the destination. What is the point of working so hard and sacrificing so much, if you cannot live in peace? Your motivation is like the wind beneath your wings, you want the right type to help you to soar not the type that will give you extreme turbulence along the way. Fear clouds your judgement and may cause you to act prematurely or delay and miss out on getting as far as you could go. Let your motivation be rooted in love and passion, let it be fuelled by purpose. Let your motivation be more than to survive, let your motivation cause you to thrive.

MY DAILY WOW AFFIRMATION

I will not be stopped by fear
I will rise above fear
I am motivated by love
I am motivated by passion
I am motivated by purpose

DAY 311

Focus on building the new not just repairing the old

. . .

There will be a time when you have to let go of the old in order to create space for the new. When something is precious to you and holds sentimental value it is easy to want to hold on to it, because it is attached to a feeling that is positive. Its personal value makes it seem worth its keep. However, the energy and resources you are using to hold on, in actual fact is causing you to miss out on greater. Although you have tried to build and repair, the justification to hold on is becoming less and less. Stop dwelling on the ruins of old. It's time to rebuild and prepare for the new. You need to create space for what is to come and reserve your resources and energy for that. Better is coming, be at peace, move on and let go.

MY DAILY WOW AFFIRMATION

I am letting go of anything that no longer adds value
I am building an amazing legacy
I am investing my energy wisely
Better things are on their way
I am working towards greatness

DAY 312

Self-care is not selfish, it's necessary

. . .

It is so important that to look after yourself. No one will know you more than you know yourself and your needs. No one occupies your mind or body. However you also have to be real with yourself. If you always say 'you are fine or ok' but it is evident that you are struggling, it is a sure sign that you have put yourself last. That you have not valued the importance of maintaining your health, mentally, spiritually or physically. And all of these areas are just as important because they make up a special part of you, Feed yourself with the right things, exercise and keep yourself active to maximise productivity and rest regularly. Especially if what you do in life involves you helping others in any way, remember you can't pour from an empty vessel. Make sure you are ok first before pouring into others.

MY DAILY WOW AFFIRMATION

I am making myself a priority
I am building myself in all areas of my life
I am maximising my productivity
I am committed to my restoration
I am being made whole and complete

DAY 313

A closed door is direction not rejection

. . .

Always be thankful for closed doors. As it is not every door that you think is a blessing, some open doors lead to confusion, delay, distractions and down roads that can be disastrous. Also take note, that only because you knocked on a door and received a response, does not mean you have to enter it, if something looks wrong, or you sense something negative, it's because something is wrong. Trust your instincts, they are there to guide you. You may not always receive the whole picture when you start on your journey. That closed door is a blessing and is there to guide you by letting you know you have to keep going. Don't stop at the first closed door, keep banging on doors until the right one opens, and you have peace to proceed. The doors that you are meant to go through will be clear and open.

MY DAILY WOW AFFIRMATION

I am grateful for the closed doors
I am thankful for being redirected
I will not be discouraged by anyone's opinion
I am made for great things
I will get to my destination

DAY 314

Grow in the midst of adversity

. . .

Growing when the atmosphere is convenient or comfortable is easy. Growing in adversity is difficult but every time you do, you grow stronger and more resilient. You are not easily shaken or phased by your environment or what is against you. Use the negativity in your life and find a way to turn them into positives. This will help you to grow, because you are building character and creating something from nothing, you are learning, becoming more stronger and wiser.

Life happens real situations come to shake your world, but use them as opportunities for development rather than being overwhelmed and consumed. The test wasn't to break you, it was for your breakthrough. Keep pressing, pushing and moving forward. As you do, the struggle becomes less of a struggle and gradually becomes easier. Things start to move and shift in your favour, what once worked against you, now works in your favour.

MY DAILY WOW AFFIRMATION

I will continue to rise above adversity
I will use adversity to grow
I am stronger than what surrounds me
I influence my surroundings
I control the atmosphere around me

DAY 315

Do not judge and do not fear being judged

. . .

Everyone has an opinion, but don't let their opinion become your reality. From a very young age like most people, you are constantly taught to assess a situation and make a judgement. However, what is rarely taught is that things change, which may make your initial judgement invalid. You are rarely told to review judgements you have made because they are usually meant to be final. But with the knowledge that things and people are forever changing, do not make a final decision that will guide permanent action. Rather constantly assess a situation and make independent decisions coupled by action. Likewise, do not be fazed by how people have judged you, you are continually changing and becoming better. Be confident and fuelled by that truth. You do not have to be limited by their opinions of you, whether good or bad, you are who you are and you are always striving to become more.

MY DAILY WOW AFFIRMATION

I will not be fazed by anyone's criticisms
I am who I am
I am getting better
I am learning and growing
I am a work in progress

DAY 316

Don't be afraid,
be inspired

. . .

Your gift will make room for you, it places you in positions and environments that you may not consider yourself to be worthy of being in. But you add something very important to that room. Own who you are called to be in this world. Do not be afraid of your skills or who doesn't like you. Let it inspire you to be more and to do more. Use it to encourage people like you that feel undeserving, let them know they too belong, they too are worthy, they too should not allow fear to hold them back. Don't be afraid to shine, someone needs your light to see and believe that it is possible. Because it is possible and you are testament of that fact. Get creative, start producing, let there be some sort of gain from either the lessons you have learned or the skill you have built.

MY DAILY WOW AFFIRMATION

I am inspired by life
I will not allow fear to hold me back
I am deserving of every blessing
My creativity will yield exciting new inventions
I will make the impossible possible

DAY 317

Let your vision be great

. . .

Set your eyes on the most brilliant, excellent vision you can think of because that is what you are becoming and forms the destination of the journey you are embarking on. It's hard to be motivated by mediocrity. But something that is world class is more appealing. If you can't see it, get creative and start imagining. It starts off as a picture but can turn into a masterpiece if you sculpt it correctly. Dream and then build, what is the worst that can happen? Even if it does not materialise you are not worse off, you just gave yourself a chance at something great. But it is more likely to materialise if you are willing to make some necessary adjustments to how your life operates now. Start being great now, start as you mean to continue, make how your vision appears to be a reality by living it out now.

MY DAILY WOW AFFIRMATION

My vision is exciting
My vision motivates me
My dreams are possible
I can do and achieve whatever I set my heart on
I am capable of amazing things

DAY 318

The greatest successes come from overcoming the biggest failures

. . .

You may lose a few battles, before you win the war, but be reminded, your ultimate goal is to win. You cannot be great without becoming worthy of the title, being great is being able to do something most people cannot do or something most people will not do. Most people will throw in the towel before trying, or failing constantly, or until the dream is realised. Only few endure multiple failures with the hope of succeeding eventually. Most people will give up waiting when what they want does not materialise within a certain timeframe. Only few will wait and keep holding on with the hope that eventually what they desire will be made available to them. The pressure to achieve after embarking on an uncommon journey will cause most people to forfeit the dream with the fear that they may not succeed. But you are not most people you are great.

MY DAILY WOW AFFIRMATION

I am an overcomer
My failures are temporary
I use my failures as stepping stones
Failure is not my final destination
I am the greatest success story

DAY 319

You have the power

. . .

You are stronger, much wiser and intelligent than you think. You have made it this far and have everything necessary to finish the journey successfully. Everything you think you lack; you actually have the power to acquire through discipline and creativity. You have the power and you also have the choice, whether to use it or not. There are problems that you have the power to solve; decisions that you have the power to make; conditions, that you have the power to change. That power is innate and is not something that is given to you externally or something that you have to fight for. You may not have the same type of power as those around you. But the more you use the power, the more it grows. The more you honour the power, the more impact it has. Use you innate gift and operate in your authority.

MY DAILY WOW AFFIRMATION

I am powerful
I make well thought through decisions
I value my gifts
I will use my gifts to empower those around me
I do not lack anything needed for my success

DAY 320

Humility comes before elevation

. . .

Be humble, elevation rarely comes just because you feel you are deserving of it. Promotion comes with perseverance and respect of the process. When you let your ego get in the way, you stop doing what is necessary to get to where you want to go. The feelings of entitlement remove your focus and energy away from working on your promotion, it instead shifts you to feeling robbed of a promotion and complaining about not being promoted. When you fuel your ego and become proud, you distance yourself from the opportunities and people that can help or to benefits that would otherwise be made available to you. Humility attracts the favour that you need to take you to where you are going, it makes you grateful and appreciative of where you are and what you have. Humility makes you value the people around you that are supporting you and causes them to continue to do just that.

MY DAILY WOW AFFIRMATION

I will remain humble
I will not allow pride to rob me of my blessings
I will strive to always be grateful
I am thankful for where I am today
I am working on progressing daily

DAY 321

You can,
so you must

. . .

Although it may look impossible, it is very possible. Although it seems like you can't, you can and therefore you must. You must strive to go where no one has been before because there are still things waiting to be discovered. You must do what has not been done before because many are waiting to hear about an experience that has never been told before. You have what is needed to make the impossible, possible. You are intelligent enough, strong enough and skilled enough to see it through to completion. Do not talk yourself out of it, this is your opportunity to meet with and fulfil purpose. It is because of the unshakeable confidence of those before you, that you are enjoying the luxuries of this day, like planes, phones, cars, the internet, to name a few. Operate in that same self-confidence that you, yes you, can and must do something extraordinarily great too. Something that lives on when you are long gone and touches the lives of many.

MY DAILY WOW AFFIRMATION

I will achieve what seems impossible
I can, therefore I will
I am bold
I am confident
I am unshakable

DAY 322

Look at the past for reference, look at the future for guidance

. . .

The past is not to condemn you and judge you for all the mistakes you have made, neither is it there as a pedestal of past achievements. The past is a reference to give you understanding on ways in which to apply lessons learned. Learn from both your past mistakes and victories, what did you do specifically that led to your achievement? When you somehow got it wrong, when and how did you miss your way? Was it because you were distracted? If so, then become more focused. Similarly, if you are using someone else's life as an example apply the same principles, use their past as a reference. And then use the future as a guide. Where do you see yourself? What will it take to get there? Are there several routes? Which route best aligns with your personality and what you can honestly commit to? Start from there.

MY DAILY WOW AFFIRMATION

My past is what I see in my memory
My future is what I see in my vision
I will trust in my future
I will use my past only as a reference
I am excited by my future wins

DAY 323

Do not dim your light let it shine

. . .

Do not forsake who you are to make others feel good about themselves. Their insecurities should not become your weakness. You have a gift within you that needs to be shared. It is like a light in darkness, that guides and gives hope. It is precious and should be valued. Do not dim the light that has been given to you, otherwise it is not fit for purpose. Instead let it shine, let it brighten someone's day, let it warm someone's heart, let it encourage someone to not give up and to keep going. Keep shining even if those around you cannot stand you, they also cannot stop you. Your light is to bring peace, your light is to destroy darkness, your light is to uncover hidden treasures. It is vital that this light shines within you and that it spreads so than it can be enjoyed by many.

MY DAILY WOW AFFIRMATION

I will let my light shine
I will not hide the greatness within me
I will not withhold my gift
My light is precious
My light is necessary

DAY 324

Your happiness is important

. . .

Your mental well-being is important. You are important and you matter. If something doesn't feel right and is making you unhappy, it is ok to remove yourself from that environment. Do not wait until you get to melting-point before doing something about it. It may be too late by that time. Being in situations where you are constantly unhappy, breaks you inside, it leaves you empty and weighed down. It can often times make you feel weak and incapable of doing what would seem like simple tasks. Do not attach your happiness to things that you cannot control because this will imprison you and cause you to make decisions that are not beneficial. Take charge of and start owning your happiness. You will find that you are more effective, that you have more clarity regarding what you want and that you are a more confident person.

MY DAILY WOW AFFIRMATION

My happiness is important
My happiness is not tied to external factors
My happiness is internal
I will remove myself from joy-killers
I will cultivate a grateful attitude

DAY 325

Do not be intimidated by the strength of others

. . .

The presence of someone's strength is not the absence of yours. You are not less because someone has strength and ability. You too have power and great skill in many areas, it is important for you to learn how to use it. Someone can be more physically stronger than you, but you can be more powerful than them in your ability to influence. Someone can be faster than you, but you can apply your intelligence to be quicker than them in getting to a destination or completing a task. It is important for you to identify the different components of yourself that make you great. Nurture and develop these components, then use them to serve you and your purpose. They heighten your gifts and put you before people of great calibre. And when you are in a room of powerful people, know it is because you are one of them.

MY DAILY WOW AFFIRMATION

No one's strength negates mine
I am still strong
I have power
I am in control of my actions
I will invest in myself

DAY 326

It always seems impossible until it is done

. . .

Nothing is impossible and that is what you must remember and believe. It's only impossible now, but who knows what possibilities tomorrow will bring. As humans we are constantly evolving and finding ways to do what seems like the impossible. Everything is possible, you just have to discover what is hidden and solve the unsolved problem. You do this by constantly trying until you get it. You do this by practicing until you are the expert. You do this by searching until you find it. That is how you make the impossible, possible. And you do not have to be a genius, expert or prodigy before it happens, in fact those very titles and accolades come once you make the achievement. And furthermore, it is not impossible for you to make the impossible happen, you just have to be committed and believe that it is already done.

MY DAILY WOW AFFIRMATION

What I'm trying to achieve is possible
I will execute my plans
I will find a way to reach my goals
I will get to my destination
I will not doubt my abilities

DAY 327

Believe in you

. . .

No one in the whole world has to believe in you and you can still do incredibly amazing things. However, if you do not believe in yourself, you are then limited from experiencing the remarkable things you could achieve. Self-belief is the driving force for will-power, without it, you have no will and you lack power. Self-belief starts from a thought-process triggered by action. Your self-belief is like an energy source, it fuels you to run that extra mile, wake up early, forsake sleep, forsake that last piece of cake or that extra piece of chicken. When you believe in the person you are becoming you are willing to do whatever it takes to get there. You begin to align yourself with thoughts that elevate you, not in an egotistical way, but in a way that builds your self-esteem. This internal attitude promotes a positive opinion of your abilities and therefore builds your confidence to actually make something happen.

MY DAILY WOW AFFIRMATION

I believe in myself
I believe in my abilities
I am gifted
I am skilled
I have a divine purpose

DAY 328

Treat yourself with care

. . .

Self-talk is inevitable, but if you are going to talk to yourself you might as well have a sensible conversation. Beating yourself up with your words, is not profitable. Have a conversation with yourself that lifts your spirit, that elevates your mood and that boosts your confidence. When it comes down to it, you are all you have, make a decision to be your best friend. Celebrate your wins, encourage yourself through your losses. Don't get into the habit of needing external validation from people. Validate yourself with words that affirm you, who you want to be and where you want to go. Be honest and real with yourself, when you are not doing so well, affirm yourself with words that will cause you to act and perform better. Fine tune your internal language, let it be reflective of the person you want to portray and become.

MY DAILY WOW AFFIRMATION

I will speak kindly to myself
I will use my inner voice to build myself
I will not speak destructively to myself
I will speak words of love
I will speak the truth

DAY 329

You were planted to grow, bloom and be fruitful

. . .

You are where you are for your growth. Do not try to speed up or skip the process. Part of growth is healing, and dealing with past hurts or pains that are unresolved. You have to decide to forgive and let go. You cannot let what happened stunt your growth even if you are justified for feeling the way you do. Justice sometimes lies in your freedom. Stop being a prisoner of un-forgiveness, be free. It is time to flourish and blossom, let the world see the beauty of who you are, let them see the product of your growth. And then see how everything you do becomes fruitful, you become more than you have ever been before. You are a source of provision, so pass on all of who you are in multiplication. It is amazing to be able to live a full life and pass on everything that you have been multiplied.

MY DAILY WOW AFFIRMATION

I am planted to grow
I will blossom
I will be fruitful
I am productive
I am effective in all my endeavours

DAY 330

Be good to yourself

. . .

Stop being your biggest critic and your own worst enemy. Love, encourage and build yourself so you don't require or expect this from anyone else. That is far too much power to give another human being, especially if you can't produce it yourself. Treat yourself with tenderness. Be patient with yourself, you will not always get things the first, second or third time around, but if you continue you will get there eventually. Coach yourself to get to where you want to go. Give yourself rewards for your accomplishments. Praise and celebrate yourself when you reach goals. You owe it to yourself to be good to yourself as you will be with you for a very long time and you are the vehicle that will take you to the destination you are striving to reach. Take good care of yourself and fill yourself up with love, be whole and be complete.

MY DAILY WOW AFFIRMATION

I am an asset

I am valuable

I am important

I will make self-care a priority in my life

I will be patient with myself

DAY 331

You manifest externally what you believe internally

. . .

Believe in the best parts of yourself, nurture and let these parts grow so they will radiate out of you like a light illuminating your worth and virtue. You can't want to be great and reach high altitudes if internally you think low of yourself and that you are incapable. The work always starts within and is validated with continual affirmation. You have to constantly check yourself to see if what you are feeling on the inside aligns with who you want to be on the outside. You can't want a great body, a nice house, well behaved children if internally you do not develop discipline, self-control and patience. What are your values? What is really important to you? Whatever it is will show in the effort you put into what you are doing. Believe in who you intend to be and what you intend to do and they will happen for you.

MY DAILY WOW AFFIRMATION

I will do internal checks regularly
I will complete the work internally
I will commit to being internally whole
I will invest in my internal transformation
I will commit to my internal restoration

DAY 332

Be your complete and authentic self

. . .

Be your truest and most authentic self. Get all the knowledge and experience you need to understand who you are and what you are meant to do to live a complete and full life. Do not emulate or copy anyone else, be yourself. You were physically engineered by creation to be unique, so by trying to be like someone else you are doing yourself an injustice. It Is ok to share similarities with someone, but never forget that you are still you, a complete and entire entity. Strive to be whole. Where there are gaps in your self-esteem, self-believe and self-love; work on filling yourself up so that you can operate at your optimum. Fuel yourself with the best of everything do not settle for worse or the last of what is left. It is important that you feed yourself with the best as that is what you will become.

MY DAILY WOW AFFIRMATION

I am whole and complete
I am authentically myself
I am unique
I am great
I am wonderful

DAY 333

It doesn't always get easier, you become better at being able to handle it

. . .

There will be times that you face challenges and you will wonder whether it will ever get easier. Sometimes it won't get easier, but you will grow stronger, wiser and more equipped to face the challenge head on. Whether it is applying more discipline, being more confident or making more of an effort than necessary, you become better at managing your expectations and ability to overcome the challenge. The importance is consistency. You can't expect to be better if you do not regularly commit to what it is that you are trying to accomplish. The more you engage in the task, the more you are able to make improvements. Each time you face the challenge, you are better equipped with an understanding of how to apply what you have learnt. And as you learn you continue to apply until you are at your best.

MY DAILY WOW AFFIRMATION

I am improving day by day
I am making progress constantly
I am developing my strength
I am becoming more knowledgeable
I am getting better daily

DAY 334

Don't worry about how, start believing it will

. . .

When you believe and take continuous action, the outcome will always shift in your favour. When you focus on the how, you build up invisible walls, mountains and hurdles. You see the difficulties and the path becomes cloudy. You do not need to see the whole picture before you take your first steps. The first steps will give you more of an understanding of which way to go next and what you must do, or who you must connect with. Your faith will be the bridge that will take you across that distance. Your faith will be the ladder you climb to get over that wall, your faith will be the hammer to break that glass ceiling. Believe that it will and that you are unstoppable, no matter the hindrance, you will always find a way through. When you believe this, you will uncover what was hidden and the path will be made clear.

MY DAILY WOW AFFIRMATION

I will execute my plans
I will achieve my goals
I will accomplish all of my undertakings
I know I will make it even if I don't know how
I am victorious

DAY 335

Stay patient and trust your journey

. . .

Do not act in haste due to your frustration of waiting. What you are waiting for is worth the wait. Also acting in haste can sabotage the rewards of waiting and being patient. There are additional gifts for being patient; you learn not to be moved by external factors, they have no bearing on your emotions or temperament, neither do you fear that you are missing out on better. Another gift is peace, being patient, gives you peace within, you have a knowledge that if something is meant for you, it will meet you where you are, at the appointed time. Life never is a straight path, but comes with many twist and turns. Don't go off course when things get tough. Stay focused and fixed on your destination. Do not be reactive, stay cool under pressure being secure in what you are waiting for is for your good.

MY DAILY WOW AFFIRMATION

I will be patient
I trust my journey
I am confident in my ability
I am being divinely guided
I have peace

DAY 336

When you believe in yourself the possibilities are infinite

. . .

When you believe in yourself the possibilities are limitless. You cannot be stopped, you are invincible. There is nothing that you cannot do, because you will always find a way to make it work, a way to get it done, the right people to help you. So, to make it through, believe in yourself. It is almost like a super power; you can do absolutely everything and anything you want to achieve, it is not impossible to do it and it is not impossible for you to do it. Take a chance on yourself, be patient with yourself, be kind to yourself, push and motivate yourself. Be self-reliant. If it is going to get done, you will be the one to do it. That doesn't mean you do not need help, it just means that you will be the one to keep the momentum and drive for accomplishment going.

MY DAILY WOW AFFIRMATION

I believe in myself
I have infinite potential
I can achieve anything I set my heart on
I am capable of achieving the impossible
I am skilled

DAY 337

No regrets in life, just lessons learned

. . .

Every lesson is a blessing, even if it came with tears, cuts, bruises, heartache, pain and maybe a bit of suffering. These lessons make you better. They are for your good and for your growth. It was a tough pill to swallow but it was what you needed to get you this far. So do not live in regret, hoping to relive past mistakes. What happened, has already past and you can only move onwards and upwards. Protect your energy from people or environments that would seek to drain you, especially if you have experienced being used and have felt like the life was sucked out of you. Protect your emotions and act intuitively with your mind intact, especially if you have been manipulated and misled, or are feeling betrayed and exposed. These lessons are birthed from experiences that are not pleasant, but they help us in the long run.

MY DAILY WOW AFFIRMATION

I am not weighed down by my past
I am free from past mistakes
I am growing and learning
I am better than who I was yesterday
I am wiser and more humble

DAY 338

Your breakthrough is on the other side of your push through

. . .

Don't quit. Hold on. Push through. Everything you have worked so hard for is on the other side of that last big push. And the harder it is to push the bigger the breakthrough. It is always when it gets most challenging that you are on to something great. This is not the time to stop. Hang on in there. Keep holding on. Do whatever it takes, dig deeper than you ever have. Reach within yourself to a place that you have never gone before. Take from the reserve, the little energy you have stored away that takes you over your highest limit, you will make it. You will breakthrough every form of resistance, everything that has held you back up until this point, but you must fight like your life depends on it. Because once you breakthrough, not only do you win but you create access for others fighting the same battle.

MY DAILY WOW AFFIRMATION

I will push through
I will get a breakthrough
I will overcome
I will accomplish greatness
I will not stop fighting

DAY 339

It is not too late to dream

. . .

It is not over until you have won. Can you see the victory? Are you anywhere close? If it is still far off, then you are still in the race. And even if you feel like the time has passed and there is no point in trying to start now, the very fact that you had the thought to start means that you need to give it a go. That dream was given to you as a divine gift, you do not know who will benefit from your act of faith. And you are not too late, you are just on time. It needed to be now. You are meeting with divine purpose by taking action on the vision that has been given to you. Do not be afraid, just believe that it will happen, and that everything will work itself out one way or another.

MY DAILY WOW AFFIRMATION

I can still make my vision a reality
I will use my time effectively
I will not lose hope
I will not be discouraged
I will not forsake my dreams

DAY 340

If it isn't serving you it's time to move on

. . .

If it doesn't help you, elevate you, add value to you, or give you peace, you need to move on. Because if it is not serving you, it is likely that it is depleting from your resources and slowly but surely destroying you. You are worth more than that and this journey that you have taken should show you that fact. You need to be surrounded by people and positioned in an environment that helps you achieve your goals. It doesn't matter which stage you are, you always need to check and analyse the purpose of anything connected to you. If it is not making the burden lighter, it is weighing you down. If it is not speeding up the process, it is bringing delay. Be real with yourself, do not be afraid to let things or people go. Get out of your comfort zone and take action.

MY DAILY WOW AFFIRMATION

I will not waste my energy on unworthy causes
My time is precious
My time is valuable
I will use my time effectively
I will use my energy to serve my purpose

DAY 341

Hope is the light at the end of the tunnel

. . .

The light at the end of the tunnel helps you to get through the darkness you are currently in. Hope sees beyond your current state, it is the reassurance that what you are going through has an end and the end is better. Find hope in whatever darkness you may find yourself in, what is the 'better thing' that you need to hold on to, to get through it? Once you find what to hope for, be confident that it will happen in due time. Walk towards it, take action constantly to get closer to it with every step you take. Even if things temporarily get worse, look to hope, being confident that you will get out of this situation as you take each step of faith towards the light and then with time you will see that light get bigger and brighter because what you once hoped for will be realised.

MY DAILY WOW AFFIRMATION

I will stay hopeful
I will keep my fire burning
I will let my light shine
I will remain confident in myself
I will hold on to my faith

DAY 342

Who you are is not stopping you, it's who you think you are not, that is

. . .

Stop thinking of yourself as less or unworthy of who you know you can be in this life. You are very intelligent, you are wise, you are kind, hard-working, confident, determined, strong, brilliant and remarkable. You were created to be all these things and you do them innately without effort. You have learnt how to navigate through life this far and are way ahead of many coming up behind you. There are things that you have had to learn that you did, and now you use these skills without much thought. There are challenges that you have faced that you overcame and because of it you can help others to overcome based on your experience. And these are just a few of many examples of how great you are. And if you are great, you are destined for greatness. But in order to attain that greatness you need to believe and understand that you are, you can and you will.

MY DAILY WOW AFFIRMATION

I will stop doubting myself
I will see myself positively
I am determined to get to my destination
I am powerful
I am capable of achieving greatness

DAY 343

Winners fail, but do not stop, winners fail, but do not quit

. . .

It is ok to fail, and keep failing and feel like a failure temporarily. But know that eventually you will succeed and because of this knowledge you cannot stop, quit or give up. You will win. That is why you have embarked on this journey and the journey does not end until you get to your destination. It may not happen when you want, but it will happen at the perfect time. When you have learnt all you need to share your skills and expertise. You may fall, but do not lay there waiting to be rescued. Get up independently, because your success is your responsibility, it is not dependent on the actions of anyone else outside of yourself. Therefore, it doesn't matter how many times you fall, what matters is that you got up and kept on going, until your steps become more certain and you become stronger.

MY DAILY WOW AFFIRMATION

I will not quit
I am a winner
I will win
I will rise above failure
I will stand back up when I fall

DAY 344

Surround yourself with the people that are going in the same direction as you

. . .

Your network is your net-worth. Make sure your circles are making you better. Surround yourself with people that are going in the same direction as you or are already there. Seek mentors, peers and partners that will support and motivate you in reaching your goals. Be accountable to these people and make them hold you to account regarding the steps you are taking to get to where you want to go. These people are your pillars when you feel weak, you can get your strength renewed when you don't feel able to continue alone. Make sure these networks challenge you to go higher and never settle or get comfortable. Make sure they keep you alert and on top of your grind. And more than anything make sure they encourage you and support your vision. It is important that they are not in competition with you or jealous of you.

MY DAILY WOW AFFIRMATION

I will surround myself with people that will lift me up
I will build my team of champions
I will establish a healthy support system
I will be an effective team player
I will connect with fellow winners

DAY 345

Success isn't just about your accomplishments but how you inspire others to accomplish also

. . .

Do people believe in their own abilities, because you showed them how you developed yours? Do they believe they can make it through because you showed them it's possible? Do they believe that they can overcome, because they saw how you overcame? If you reach your goal, but no one knows your story, the impact may be limited. However, if your accomplishments inspire more accomplishment and achievement, then your success is multiplied and there is no limit to how much it can reach those that you are physically unable to access. Your story can travel where your feet have not tread. Your will-power, determination and resilience can cause a response from someone on the edge of giving up. You can prolong and save a life, just through sharing your story. And there is no greater success than that which brings freedom and hope to so many for generations to come.

MY DAILY WOW AFFIRMATION

I will endeavour to inspire
I will share my story
I will make a positive impact to those around me
I will influence constructively
I am a blessing

DAY 346

People pour into you, or they drain you

. . .

If the goal is to win, make sure you pick the right team. Having able bodies to make up numbers, but that don't put the work in won't cut it. Choose wisely, as this can impact how far you go and the pace in which you get there. Is your team pouring into you, or draining you? Do you feel energised and supported by your circle? Or do you feel, lonely, tired and weighed down? If it is the latter, you have to change your team immediately as you will end up ineffective. If you are ineffective how can you become the person you are desiring to be? If you are ineffective how can you get to your destination? Your team are a vital part of your journey and they need to be the right people, with a similar mind set, work ethic and acumen to achieve the very best in life.

MY DAILY WOW AFFIRMATION

I will remove myself from people that drain me
I will not let people take advantage of me
I will use my discernment
I will build respectful boundaries
I will stand strong in who I am

DAY 347

No matter the obstacle, challenge or loss, let them act as motivation

. . .

If you were not such a fret or a force to be reckoned with there will be no need to oppose you. But because what you carry is so great, it scares some people, so they want to see you fail. Life also wants to test whether you are worthy of the position you seek. The only way to progress is to proceed forward with full force. Do not be phased by what is ahead of you that seems to be against you, you have everything within you that is necessary to overcome. Use the emotion you feel to fuel and motivate you to keep on fighting. You are more than worthy of all the benefits that life has to offer, so go for it without apology. Do not be moved, shaken or frustrated by the current struggle, be motivated to win and want it more than ever before.

MY DAILY WOW AFFIRMATION

I am motivated by life
I will not let obstacles discourage me
I will rise to the challenge
I am an overcomer
I am a warrior

DAY 348

Self-discipline begins with the mastery of your mind

. . .

Master your mind, become master of your life. Your mind can be a place of solitude or a waging war against your soul. It can strengthen you or wreck you. It is important to train your mind to serve you so that you are empowered to face anything that comes your way. Build your mind up by fuelling it with food that will nourish it and help it to grow. Give your mind rest so that you do not overwork it, this can occur when you overthink and therefore become tired and overwhelmed. Take your mind away from things that will occupy space but add no value to who you are or who you are becoming. Let your mind challenge you and push you to limits you never thought you could reach. Let your mind be a home of your vision, nesting it until it is ready to take off and soar.

MY DAILY WOW AFFIRMATION

I am mastering my mind
I have control over my thoughts
I choose thoughts that will build me up
I devote myself to self-control
I commit to self-discipline

DAY 349

Start now to advance later

. . .

Start and start now, take one step at a time, you do not have to change the world in a day. But when you start, start with the aim to finish. Start with the aim to complete what you want to accomplish well. Do not start several things at once. Start with the hope to build on a great foundation, something that will last and outlive you. Be committed to continuous improvement. Don't wait to get or have more, don't wait to reach a particular place, start where you are and with what you have now. Whatever provisions you need for your journey will be made available to you as and when you need it. If you do not start you will never get the help you need, waiting on someone to give you that push. That person may never come. Do not let excuses keep you from starting or executing your dreams.

MY DAILY WOW AFFIRMATION

I will not neglect small beginnings
I will start where I am
I will not be overwhelmed by what lies ahead
I will commit to the journey
I will finish my course

DAY 350

Rise above the storm

. . .

The only way to get through the storm is to rise above it. Be better, greater and bigger than any storm in your life. It cannot overcome you when you are over it. The storm may seek to distract you and overpower you, it doesn't want to see you grow or see you prosper. But the storm does not dictate your destiny, you do. You have the power to silence the storm and halt it's activity, you just need the confidence to believe in yourself enough and take the necessary action. Always remember the storm is temporary. It will not last forever, it is but for a short while that it rages against you seeking to consume you, but it won't and it can't. The storm cannot break you. Do not let the storm wreck you or disorientate you. Be mindful of your bearings and stay focused on where you are heading to.

MY DAILY WOW AFFIRMATION

I will rise above the storm
I will overcome challenges
I will conquer the problem
I am stronger than the obstacle
My faith will move any mountain

DAY 351

Failure is not fatal

. . .

Be humble when you have in abundance and ambitious when you lack. Times and seasons change, always be hopeful for tomorrow and grateful for today. If you fail today know that, your failure is not final, it is not a destination, it is not where everything stops. And failure won't kill you so don't allow fear of failure to stop you. There is life after you fail. There are journeys to make, people to connect with, lives to impact, goals to reach. Don't stay stuck at where you fell short, let the fact that you are not where you need to be, motivate you to keep on going, let it propel you forward. There is so much to be achieved, so the sooner you get over the shame of not making it the first time round, the sooner you get another chance of making it work, this time around.

MY DAILY WOW AFFIRMATION

Failure is not fatal
Failure is not final
I will breakthrough
I will overcome
I will rise above my challenges

DAY 352

It's not about having the time it is about making the time

. . .

Honestly there will always be time to be busy, in fact you can even find yourself busy doing nothing. Don't be one of those people who has no command over their time or schedule. Be active and intentional with your time, actively make the time to do the things you love. Be intentional about using your time, doing the things that will propel you forward and closer to fulfilling your vision as well as the things that will bring value to your life. This includes spending time with family and friends. Time can often seem scarce when you fill it with stuff to do for doing sake. Make every moment count. As it is often said, do not count the days, but make the days count. Make sure that you spend your time in a way that serves your daily goals and ultimately your purpose.

MY DAILY WOW AFFIRMATION

I take control of my time
I value my time
I use my time wisely
I do not waste time
I show up on time

DAY 353

Never give up on something you really want, it's difficult to wait, but worse to regret

. . .

It's so tempting to call it quits when you have tried and tried and tried again but it seems like you have not even scratched the surface or come close to where you want to be.

Don't get discouraged, for the ones that don't give up the reward is far greater than the struggle it took to get there.

In addition, you gain life skills that set you up for any other challenge that comes your way, such as discipline, perseverance, resilience, hope, endurance, strength and patience. Your goal is worth your continuous efforts in pursuit of achievement. You have the right to keep going, you are permitted to go full force ahead, relentlessly without regression. Go all the way. Do not wait on anyone or anything. You have everything within you to win and make it across to the other side. You won't regret not giving up.

MY DAILY WOW AFFIRMATION

I will not give up
I will not throw in the towel
I will be patient
I will keep fighting
I will get through this trial

DAY 354

If you want it to last you have to put in the work

. . .

Consistency is key, if you want something you have to work for it. And once you have it, don't walk in fear that it will be gone tomorrow. Nurture it. More often than not, maintaining great heights of success or achievement is more challenging than getting there in the first place. Preserve and maintain your blessings, this will likely involve you making some changes in your life and getting out of your comfort zone. But this is an essential part of success. Staying on top, guarding your position, protecting your assets, will require you to operate at a whole new level and with a different group of people. These people will give insight on how to operate at this level of greatness and maintain it. You will have to dig deeper and in some ways it may feel like you are starting afresh, because this is new and you have a few things to learn.

MY DAILY WOW AFFIRMATION

I will remain consistent
I will commit to the work
I will work hard
I am intelligent
I have divine ability

DAY 355

You have what it takes to win

· · ·

You have already won and that is the mind-set that you have to have, to beat every opponent. You are not competing with them to win, you are just taking the necessary steps to get to your destination. Keep your eyes fixed. You are strong enough to run the extra mile, wake up that much earlier, go at it for that much longer. Because you know that all the work you are putting in is instilling the level of self-discipline that only the greats have. Most people would have given up by now, but you are not most people, you are extraordinary with remarkable skill and talent. You have what it takes, because you will do whatever it takes, and you will do whatever it takes because you know the value of the purpose you carry. You can't compromise your best and settle for mediocrity because that is not who you were called to be.

MY DAILY WOW AFFIRMATION

I am a winner
I will win
I am skilled
I am capable of accomplishing great things
I have everything I need to reach my goals

DAY 356

Don't miss out on the great for the quick and easy

. . .

Nothing great in this life comes without a cost, but the value you place on it far outweighs the price you have to pay. When something is quick and easy it rarely endures for long; just as quickly as you received it, is how quickly it is gone. However, when you work tirelessly to see something through to the end, paying close attention to detail and attending to its development, the rewards are endless, and it lasts for long enough to appreciate many times over. Never forfeit the great for a quick fix, it is never worth it. However, when you persevere and wait, it is always worth it because the rewards overshadow any effort or work you put into it. It can be difficult, however if you stay focused and keep your eyes fixed on the vision you will realise your goal well before you anticipated.

MY DAILY WOW AFFIRMATION

I will be patient
I will not act in haste
I am not lazy
I am hardworking
I am productive

DAY 357

Be secure in your ability to adapt and grow

. . .

Don't underestimate your ability to change and adapt in a way that serves you and where you are going. Be more confident that if circumstances change, you will cope by adapting your method or technique. You will not be dumbfounded or confused but you will find another way to make it work. There is so much more that you can do, don't let your limited belief in your abilities hinder you. You do not know what your limits are, until they are challenged and even then, you can push past your limits and end up surprising yourself. Even if people change on you and do not appear to be reliable, although you can distance yourself from them, do not burn bridges, you never know when you will come across that same person again. And when you do, they could have completely changed and learnt from their mistakes and so could you.

MY DAILY WOW AFFIRMATION

I am constantly evolving
I am developing my skills
I am growing daily
I am making good progress
I am able to adapt when required

DAY 358

Spend your time with people that genuinely want to see you win

. . .

Don't waste time on people that just want to be around you to keep up with what you are doing. They are using you as a measuring stick to determine their own success or lack of it. They are secretly competing with you, which is not healthy for you or them. Keep away from these people. It is not always easy to recognise the difference between these people and those that are genuinely for you, but if they do not add value to your progression, or make you better in anyway shape or form, but constantly enquire about every detail of what you are doing and then use it to compare that to what they are doing or have achieved, then it is likely these people are not really for you. Your success makes them uncomfortable and that is no fault of your own. But you cannot be around that sort of energy.

MY DAILY WOW AFFIRMATION

I will value my support system
I will invest time in my team
I will fight for those who champion me
I will care for my loved ones
I will cherish my inner circle

DAY 359

It's not about who you know, it's about who knows you

...

Continue to work on and invest in yourself so it's clear what you bring to the table and who should sit there. When you add value, people will headhunt you and seek to meet with you. Therefore, seek to add value to the lives of people around you, do not be focused on what you can get or what they can offer you. What is it that you have to give? How can you help and assist them? Are you a solution to a problem? Work on these areas. Be someone that when people are in your presence, they leave better than they were before they met you. You will be honoured for who you are and the way you make people feel special and precious by just spending time with you. Everything you do, do with excellence, take pride in the work you produce and the service you provide, let it be world-class.

MY DAILY WOW AFFIRMATION

I am worth knowing
I will be sought after
I am connecting with the right people
I will attract favour
The right doors will open for me

DAY 360

The test was not designed to expose your weakness, but to unveil your strength

. . .

You are developed through pressure, strengthened by trials, made wiser by lessons. Each test is to show you where you are, how well you are doing and if you have improved. You may notice you are less angry and more patient, but you still need to work on your execution of tasks and stop procrastinating. If you were not tested, you may be oblivious to how you are actually doing and begin to regress. You should always work on improving on where you were before. You do not need to do this in isolation, if necessary get the help that you need. Get guidance on how to be even stronger and more equipped to face the next test of life. Never get comfortable in the position you are in now, there is always room for improvement, and you must always improve if you want to be the best.

MY DAILY WOW AFFIRMATION

I will pass the test
I am stronger than I think
I will supersede my expectations
I am developing my weaknesses into strengths
I am capable and skilled

DAY 361

You may have to lose for a moment to win for a lifetime

. . .

Don't be afraid to take some losses along the way, even if the ultimate goal is to win. Keep working on winning. And even when you win focus on how to keep on winning. When you are close to winning do not stop doing what you have been doing. Stay focused. Keep on training and working hard. The same hard work that got you there will be the same hard work needed to keep you there. Keep on putting in the work and the hours. The numbers will speak for themselves when the time is right. Don't let any losses discourage you. The loss is temporary, you can still win. Do not let the loss define you. You are not a loser, you haven't been counted out or side-lined, you are more important now, more than ever before. You are a winner, so do what you do best and find a way to win.

MY DAILY WOW AFFIRMATION

I will not be hindered by temporary losses
I will not be stopped
In the end I win
I am victorious
I am a champion

DAY 362

The will to win is important, but the will to prepare is vital

. . .

Preparation is a significant part of winning. Everything that happens before you win is determining if you are going to win or not. Are you doing what it takes to win? Have you made a plan of action of how you are going to win and what you are going to do once you have won? Winning is great, but the disciplines you learn along the way to winning is what takes you across the finish line. You can win but you have to make the necessary preparation to win, you have to make adjustments in your life, so that your appetite is that of a winner, your conduct is that of a winner, your mannerisms are that of a winner. All of this takes practice. You will have to constantly review your methodology because the technique you used to win before may not be the technique needed for the next challenge.

MY DAILY WOW AFFIRMATION

I will commit to constant preparation
I will prepare to win
I will accomplish my dreams
I am disciplined
I am focused

DAY 363

To win big, you sometimes have to take big risks

. . .

What are you willing to risk to win big? A few nights of sleep? Sacrificing your morning lie-in for early mornings? A couple of missed social events? Loneliness and isolation? Whatever the risk, make sure the results are well worth it, so that you can keep your eye on the prize at all times and so that you do not live in regret. You are a worthy investment and you are worth the risk it will take to get you to where you are going. What is there to lose? Even if you do not see a win immediately. Keep on going at it until you get a return on your investments, you will reap the rewards in due time, and you will be so grateful that you took a chance on yourself. You will be happy that you did not wait on someone else but that you took action on yourself for yourself.

MY DAILY WOW AFFIRMATION

I am willing to take a chance on myself
I am worth the risk
I am valuable
I am a worthy investment
I risk big to win big

DAY 364

Your opinion is what matters

. . .

No one's opinion matters when it comes to your life as much as yours. What people think of you, does not matter. And their opinions will constantly change so you cannot use this as a point of reference for anything you want to consider in applying to your life where opinions are concerned. What you think of yourself is important because that will shape the person you are and hope to be. Therefore, make sure your opinion of your life and the decisions you make are positive. And if they currently are not positive make the necessary arrangements that are required to make your opinions of yourself reflective of who you want to be in this life. You cannot have anyone else's life, so you have to make the most out of your own. Keep affirming yourself until you become the person you will be proud of.

MY DAILY WOW AFFIRMATION

I am the author of my destiny
My opinion is important
My belief is important
I will nurture my creativity
I will express my faith in action

DAY 365

Jump higher to reach the bar, don't lower the bar to make the jump

. . .

You have the ability to push through your limits, but it requires for you to step out of your comfort zone. When you are willing to leave behind the safety net, you are able to explore parts of life that you can only imagine. You can do this gradually so that you are not overwhelmed and overcome by anxiety. Keep the bar raised, once you can reach it, raise it higher. The more you push your boundaries, the more you are able to push past your limitations which increases your confidence to do it more and more. This takes you to greater heights and deeper depths of self-discovery and achievement. When you learn to be comfortable being uncomfortable, fear cannot hold you or stop you. You are able to perform on a whole new level without giving it a thought.

MY DAILY WOW AFFIRMATION

I am not limited
I overcome my challenges
I will not be hindered
I will break boundaries
I will break records

My Daily Words of
Wisdom Top-up Days

$\longrightarrow$

Be committed not just curious

. . .

Be committed. And keep committing until you see your vision realised. There is a difference between interest and commitment. When you're interested in doing something, you do it only when it's convenient for you. When you are committed to something, you accept no excuses, you do what is needed regardless of how you feel. If you are embarking on any venture it is important that you are committed before starting, as it is your commitment that will see you through to the end. Commitment is important and likewise your team also need to be committed, you need to know that they are in it for the long haul. Are they going to see it through to the end or give up at the first sign of difficulty? If it is the latter, they are not committed and you have to let them go.

MY DAILY WOW AFFIRMATION

I am committed to my vision
I am excited about reaching my destination
I know I will win
I am dedicated to my success
I will be faithful to see my work through to the end

If you don't go after what you want, you will never get it

. . .

You have to be relentless when it comes to you achieving your goals. Step out of your comfort zone and remove all restrictions. It is time to perform and apply all the work you have been putting in behind the scenes. You have to go for everything you want ruthlessly. Your life and the turn it takes is on the line and is depending on you to make the right moves. You have to put yourself out there and go for what you want, you cannot be passive. If you do not search, you still won't find what you are looking for, if you do not ask the answer will still be no, if you do not knock the door will still be shut. You have to go for what you want.

Be willing to be active and see the whole world move for you. It may not be easy, but that does not mean it is impossible.

MY DAILY WOW AFFIRMATION

I will boldly pursue my goals
I will obtain the reward for my hard work
I will keep working until I accomplish my dreams
I am a go getter
I am diligent

Be a willing student at all times

. . .

Every new level requires you to be a student, be an exceptional student of life. Study and seek not only to know, but to understand and in perfecting your understanding seek to teach, this prepares you for the next level. There is always something to learn and always something to teach. Ask the right questions to lead you to the right answers. Be inquisitive. Be an active student that wants to solve problems, not a passive student that can't translate the knowledge they have acquired and apply it to their lives. Every lesson you learn is so that you can apply it when needed. You will not always know when you will need to apply the knowledge you have gained from a lesson learnt, so always be ready and willing to act. This increases the value you add to any team; someone who is willing and able.

MY DAILY WOW AFFIRMATION

I am committed to learning
I am devoted to my personal development
I am a student of life
I am getting better through constant study
I am mastering my craft

YOU DID IT!

You made it this far. And I can't express how excited I am for your future and the wonderful things that will manifest because of your diligence.

This is not the end, this is just the beginning of more great things to come. I hope you will continue to carry me along with you on your journey. Let's stay connected, keep me up to date with your endeavours and get more information on tools that will help you by visiting the website **www. mydailywordsofwisdom.com**.

If this book has helped you in anyway please share it with as many people as you can, so that they can have the same experience.

I'd also like to know your thoughts on the book, please write a positive review so that people can get a real opinion on how the book may be useful to them too. You can do this by reviewing the book on online through the website.

Printed in Great Britain
by Amazon